Dealer's Thesaurus

6,000 Ways to Describe

Books & Historical Paper

Lynn Vigeant, Editor

Maps of Antiquity, Inc.
Montclair, N. J.

Printed in the United States of America.
on acid free paper

Library of Congress Catalog Card Number 93-91497
ISBN 0-9636914-0-6

Maps of Antiquity, Inc.
P.O. Box 569
Montclair, N.J. 07042
201-744-4364

10, 9, 8, 7, 6, 5, 4, 3, 2, 1
First Edition

INTRODUCTION

When I began to write my first catalog, I struggled to find the right words to describe what I had to sell. I combed other dealers' catalogs looking for phrases I could use. I searched in vain for a book that would help me through this difficult stage.

I spent hours wondering how to describe faults I would encounter. Describing the content of a map was particularly challenging. I quickly learned that collecting useful phrases on index cards when I came across them was more efficient than searching for a phrase to fit the situation at a given moment. I had cards labeled stains, tears, color, and edition. There was a card for praise and another for mapmakers. When I needed a phrase, I turned to the index cards and found several to choose from.

By the time my first catalog was finished I had almost one hundred index cards filled with useful phrases. I called them my *Dealer's Thesaurus*. When I finished my second catalog, I was convinced of the usefulness of this idea. Then it occurred to me to expand it further and publish it. The result is this book. I hope it makes your catalog writing easier. Your comments and suggestions for improvement will be welcome. They may be incorporated into an enlarged edition some day.

PURPOSE. The purpose of this book is to provide dealers, collectors and writers with a variety of phrases to describe antiquarian books, prints and other historical paper which they can use to enliven their catalogs, quotes and conversations. Listings are intended to be suggestive of the possibilities rather than comprehensive.

An effort has been made to provide comments in proportion to their usefulness to the target audience. Therefore categories which describe the physical aspects of books and historical paper such as bindings and faults are abundant and quite thorough, while comments which describe authors and writing styles are only a sampling of what could be said.

ARRANGEMENT. Phrases which apply only to books, maps or prints appear in their own sections. Phrases which can apply to more than one category are listed under the General Section. Maps are in a separate section even though they are prints because there are so many phrases which apply just to them. To get the most out of this book a user should become acquainted with the General Section as well as the specific sections which apply to their areas of interest. A Table of Contents and an Index are provided to help the user locate phrases.

ACKNOWLEDGEMENTS

I dedicate this book to Richard Vigeant, my husband, whose encouragement made my business, first as a book dealer, and then as a map dealer possible. He loves the books and maps as much as I do. His knowledge of history and geography has been invaluable. He encouraged me through the lean times and didn't complain when all my sales were used to acquire more inventory.

This book has benefited greatly from the help of Martha Calkins of Book Heaven who spent hours extracting phrases from books and catalogues. She helped me keep my sanity and made it fun to sort through a sea of incomplete sentences. This would be a very different book without her able assistance.

I owe a special thank you to College Women's Club of Montclair who introduced me to the world of old books when I worked as a volunteer sorting and pricing books for their annual book sale; and to the AB Bookmen Seminar staff who taught me the book business; and to Dick and Dottie Fitch who taught me how the map business was different; and to Jennifer Larson, of Yerba Buena Books, whose valuable review led to significant corrections; and to Paul Mahoney, of Old Map Gallery, for his encouragement and suggestions; and to all the book and map dealers whose catalogues were searched for useful phrases; and to Dante, my cat, who kept me company through the long hours at the computer and at my desk.

Lynn Vigeant,
Editor

Contents

GENERAL

BOOKS

AUTHOR

PRINTS

MAPS

General

ACCURACIES

a precise rendering
exact in every detail
makes every effort to be a reliable scientific document
remarkably accurate

AGE

a piece of vintage
a splendid relic
age confers value upon it
documenting an early stage in the development of...
from the era before photography was common
short-lived
shown at the transitional stage
stood the test of time
the absence of... indicates that this was issued before...
the subject is quite antique in character

ARRANGEMENT

exceptionally well-organized
in a totally random fashion
arranged in chronological order
divided equally into four parts
divided into many subcategories
includes major sections on...
not arranged in any particular order
the text is arranged in a most effective manner

AUTHENTICITY

a certificate of authenticity accompanies this...
authentic antiquarian

authenticity is questionable
every detail is as described by...
genuine and concise
purports to be... but actually...
the authenticity of this was personally confirmed
the charmingly idiosyncratic style is as much a guarantee of authenticity as is the signature
the general tenor of the document speaks to its authenticity

BUSINESS - BILLING

first-time customers please supply suitable trade references
persons ordering for the first time are requested to pay in advance
persons unknown to us should submit credit references
possession of title in the item remains with the dealer until the invoice is paid in full

BUSINESS - DEALER DISCOUNTS

dealers please inquire about discounts
dealers' discount is reciprocal
discounts apply only to bona fide dealers ordering on their letterhead

BUSINESS - GUARANTEES

all items guaranteed to be genuine
authenticity of all items unconditionally guaranteed
authenticity guaranteed or purchase price will be refunded without time limit
fully guaranteed to be authentic and complete
guaranteed original as described
we warranty authenticity for a period of 5 years from date of sale

BUSINESS - INSTITUTIONS

institutions may request deferred billing
libraries will be billed to suit their ordering procedures and budgetary requirements
we are proud to help build reference library collections

BUSINESS - ORDERING

a call beforehand might save you some aggravation
a complete list is available upon serious inquiry
alternate choices are recommended
call to reserve this piece
I suggest a call to be first to reserve this scarce item
if you're considering this one, call promptly; it won't last long
it is advisable to order early
many late orders filled
send $... for complete prospectus
serious inquiries only, please
terms are as usual
we have duplicates of some titles

BUSINESS - PRICE

affordable
another bargain for the collector
at a price that can fit most budgets
at published price
due to the uncertainty of the source the price is only...
individually priced but offered in a group for $
many selling for much more
may be had on a limited budget
my ignorance may be your bliss
neat item and price
not an attractive copy and priced accordingly
offered at $ for the pair
price reflects condition
residents of... please include ..% sales tax
should sell for..., but yours for...
this won't last long at this price
very reasonably priced
you'll like this price

BUSINESS - RETURNS

all items are considered to be shipped on approval
any item found to be unsatisfactory may be returned within a reasonable length of time
authorized returns will receive full refund or credit
full 30 day return privilege for any reason
if you are dissatisfied, you may return it within seven days
if you're not completely satisfied simply return it
please advise by phone if returning an item
please return anything found to be at odds with our description
prior notice of returns is appreciated
refunds will be made as soon as the item is back in our hands
returnable, but you won't want to
returnable within one week of receipt
returns must be insured for full value at customer's expense
sent on approval, but presumed to be sold if not promptly returned
you have the privilege of returning an item

BUSINESS - SHIPPING

add $ to defray cost of shipping
all sales are subject to shipping charges
carefully packed and properly insured
customers outside the U.S. will be invoiced for shipping
include $ for shipping and insurance per item
items shipped in state are subject to sales tax
merchandise will be shipped promptly upon receipt of payment
no delivery charges unless noted
on orders less than $200 add $3 for shipping and handling
our shipping expense will be added to the invoice
please allow three to five weeks for shipping
postage and insurance charges are included on all pre-paid sales
shipping is by UPS unless other arrangements are made
shipping is available by Federal Express, UPS, or post office

CAVEATS

a respectable copy, but...
despite these defects

fragile little item
it should be borne in mind that...
nevertheless, a fine example of...
nicer than it sounds
otherwise clean
the best condition that one could hope for
unexamined out of frame
used but not abused

COLLECTIBLE

a "must have"
a show piece to enhance your collection
a unique opportunity to add to your collection
an enthusiastically collected offering
an iconographic treasure
certainly a high spot in any collection
cornerstone to any collection
for passionate collectors
for the serious collector
invaluable to collectors
it is the cornerstone "must" for any collector
part of an acclaimed collection
represents perhaps the ultimate acquisition for the collector
the ultimate collectible

COLLECTIONS

a collector's collection
a diverse collection
a renowned collection of more than 400 items
a virtually complete collection
an almost unrivaled collection
an excellent research collection
an outstanding archive
copies have long been held by older libraries
for sale as a collection only
hoarded and displayed
included in one of the world's great collections

includes substantial holdings in such related areas as...
perhaps a unique collection
the best collection in private hands
the collection incorporates...
the definitive collection of...
this superb collection was purchased en masse
variety is the key word in describing this collection

COLOR - ADDED

background tint subsequently added
contemporary color
neatly colored by a former owner
with handsome later coloring

COLOR - BY HAND

all but one hand-colored
colored by hand under the supervision of...
delicate shading to the bright hand coloring
early and rather simple hand coloring
engravings hand-colored with superlative technical proficiency
exquisitely hand colored
full hand coloring with minor soiling
original hand highlighting
plates hand-colored and signed by the colorist
printed in color by hand

COLOR - ORIGINAL

beautiful original color throughout
copies were available uncolored and colored
original color by publisher
original highlight color
original lively brilliance
with fine coloring richly heightened in gold

COLOR - PRAISE

a perfect blend of material and color
an amazingly effective use of color

beautifully shaded
colors are bright and lively
considered to have the best color
exceptionally bright and vivid
eyecatching pastels
fully and attractively colored
handsomely marked with blues
harmonious blending of pink, red and purple
imparts unsurpassed color and texture
lush pinks
most finely detailed and beautifully colored
striking bicolor
tastefully colored
the key to emotional feeling and warmth
the original color is expecially vivid
unbelievable range of colors
well colored with opaque colors
with full, rich tones

COLOR - STYLE

bold use of color
clear washes of pale color
colors are muted
contains some tinting
glows with riotous color
gold and purple abound throughout
in differing pastel colors
in predominant hues of blue and black
mellow color scheme
pink-red speckles
possessing full, rich tonal range
primitive coloring
subtle tones
varicolored
warm peach blends

COLOR - UNCERTAIN

giving the appearance of hand coloring
it is possible that fewer copies than stated were hand-colored
likely hand coloring
outline hand color, perhaps original

COLORS - BLACK

ebony, jet

COLORS - BLACK AND WHITE

a dull achromatic affair
a winterland of unrelieved black and white
an uncolored impression

COLORS - BLUE

aquamarine, azure, cerulean, cobalt, ice, indigo, midnight, navy, peacock, royal, powder, sea, sky, teal, ultramarine

COLORS - BROWN

chestnut, chocolate, cinnamon, coffee, mink, mocha, oak, sepia, taupe, tobacco, umber, walnut

COLORS - BEIGE

autumn, bisque, brick, clay, burlap, clay, flagstone, ginger, heather, mahogany, rust, tawny, terra cotta, wheat, woodtone

COLORS - GRAY

battleship, charcoal, felt, flannel, putty, sand, silver, slate, steel

COLORS - GREEN

apple, chartreuse, emerald, forest, grass, ivy, jade, kelly, leaf, lime, mint, olive, parrot, viridian, yellowish

COLORS - LIGHT

clear, dark, iridescent, lustre, translucent, transparent

COLORS - METALLIC
bright, cool, copper, bronze, fluorescent, glossy, glowing, gold, silver, pewter, shiny, smooth

COLORS - NEUTRAL
antique, bleached, bone, buff, cork, cream, champagne, eggshell, hemp, ivory, mist neutral, oyster, pearl, vanilla

COLORS - ORANGE
coral, peach, poppy, pumpkin, salmon, terra cotta

COLORS - PINK
blush, flesh, rose, shell

COLORS - PURPLE
amethyst, cadmium, grape, imperial, lavendar, lilac, magenta, maroon, mauve, mulberry, orchid, periwinkle, violet, wine

COLORS - QUALITY
brilliant, clear, dark, deep, fresh, frosted, grayed, hot, intense, ...ish, ...like, lustre, midtone, neon, refreshing, rich, soft, strong, tint, true, vibrant

COLORS - RED
berry, carmine, cherry, chinese, cranberry, crimson, henna, raspberry, rose, rosy, ruby, scarlet

COLORS - WHITE
arctic, igloo, pure, lily, titanium, zinc

COLORS - YELLOW
blond, canary, citron, citrus, golden, honey, honeysuckle, jasmine, lemon, marigold, mustard, ochre, sunshine

COMPARISON
almost indistinguishable from...
comparable to the work of...

compares favorably with the best
comparison is inapplicable and will not be attempted
corresponds very closely to...
difficult to compare to modern counterparts
done in the same manner as...
draws an analogy with...
evokes numerous comparisons between his work and that of...
in a style similar to that of...
interesting results might arise from a comparison between...
is frequently compared to...
known for its resemblance to...
not the slightest differentiation between them
serves the same purpose as...
shows a curious resemblance to...
shows similarities in tone and format to...
similar in style, and a worthy successor to...
similar in appearance to
surpasses others
the style in some ways parallels that of...
the style is of the same blood as...
typical of its kind
very much like those from...

COMPARISON PRAISE

a much more substantial and interesting work than...
above the norm
an enlarged and more elaborate version
better, if not the best
compares favorably to...
compares well with the past
greatly improved
is worthy to rank with...
more desirable than others
much more ambitious than...
much more familiar than...
nothing equaling it has ever been found
quite similar to... but better

quite unlike the ordinary
rivals similar publications of the time
the best of this genre
unexcelled if not unequaled
very much better than before
worthy to rank with the works of...

COMPLETENESS

a decisive and complete presentation
apparently complete as issued
everything is here
includes... which is frequently missing
rarely found complete
unabridged
unrivaled for its completeness
unusually extensive

CONDITION - BEST

a bright, superior copy
a flawless copy
an absolutely splendid copy
an excellent copy
essentially perfect
exceptionally nice copy
extremely bright and fresh overall
fresh as the day it was printed
in extra fine condition
in immaculate condition
in impeccable condition
in virtually mint condition
it seems virtually never to have been used
near mint, need we say more?
none finer
rare in this exemplary condition
seldom seen in anything approaching such pristine condition
sparkling copy

superb condition
virtually as new
with no wear, faults, or blemishes whatsoever

CONDITION - BETTER

a much nicer copy than is usually encountered
appears to be typical if not better than most
better than usually seen
in much better condition than is usually found
one of the finer
remarkably clean and free from the customary offsetting
uncommonly fine

CONDITION - GOOD

a pleasant copy
all about very good or better
attractive throughout
complete and scarce but unremarkable in terms of condition
condition very good overall
crisp and fresh
entirely sound
free of foxing
generally clean, fresh and bright
generally very good to fine, particularly as to...
generally well preserved
in a remarkable state of preservation
in agreeable condition
just about fine
nice copy, nearly fine
overall complete and sound
quite clean and bright except for normal marginal toning
quite remarkable condition
rather attractive overall
reasonably bright overall
retains its freshness even now
uniformly clean and attractive
with all the old lettering intact

CONDITION - GOOD UNCOMMON

a remarkable survival in any condition
an unusually clean copy
distinguished by the very fine condition of this fragile item
in remarkably fresh condition
rarely found this complete
scarce in this condition
virtually unheard of in this condition

CONTRAST

a dramatic polarization
a quintessential counterpart to...
careful study reveals differences
clearly differentiated from the others by...
differing greatly from the work of...
differs significantly from previous works
differs substantially from...
excitingly different compared to others from the same period
one is struck by the difference in quality
puts less emphasis on... than...
should not be confused with...
similar but not identical to...
there are few parallels to be found
unlike many of its imitators
very similar to... but without...

CRITICISM

a biased examination
a crude piece of work
a largely regressive work
a little too much
a scathing indictment
a somewhat labored imitation
a vacuous view
by no means comprehensive
detracts from the overall appearance
eye-glazingly hypnotic

eye-glazingly hypnotic
fails to pull it off
fatally flawed
generally lacks refinement
harsh and unpleasing
has done a tremendous disservice
has its problematical elements
hovers somewhere between bland and offensive
its virtues are not obvious
lacks flavor
lacks flow
less than ideal
mercilessly overstated
not wholly satisfying
notably unimaginative
ornate and complicated
promises so much and fails to deliver
self-consciously naive
somehow gone awry
something is missing
stupifyingly dull
there is little new material here
this work struck a sour note
undistinguished and poorly designed
worthy of scant attention

CRITICIZED

came under immediate attack
generated an outraged reaction
generated little critical commentary
it was damned by the press
the subject of considerable public controversy
what praise it garnered was unwarranted

DATE

a notable production of the late nineteenth century
copyright 1850 but published 1853

poised to enter the year of the...
printed in 1920 and very uncommon
produced around the middle of the nineteenth century
produced on the occasion of...
published in 1806 although it still carries the original publication date of 1800
published separately at various dates
published soon after event depicted
the presence of... establishes the date as...
undated but published in 18..

DATE - UNCERTAIN

circa 1900, no date given
the date must be inferred from other evidence
the only key to the date placing it before 18... is

DECEPTION

a fabrication in an otherwise accurate report
an altogether untrustworthy account
deliberately erroneous
it is generally thought to be a fabrication
less real than it has been made out to be
one of the most successful hoaxes of its time
purports to be
the facts are misrepresented
there is no evidence to support...

DETAIL

a good trivia question
a lively, multi-faceted record
a plethora of detail
copious detail is depicted
full to the point of bursting with detail
gave inordinate attention to fine detail
gives a kaleidoscopic view
honestly observed details
in harrowing detail

meticulous portrayal of detail
mind-boggling detail
minutely describes...
stuffed with happy details
superbly detailed
the detail goes well beyond that which is normally seen
tightly compressed details
unremitting attention to every aspect
went to great pains to delineate all useful information
with details too numerous to include here
with meticulously observed detail

DIFFERENT

a rare and curious piece
an unusual approach
distinctively different
unusual for the period
weird and wonderful
with a peculiar charm

FACSIMILES

a complement to the original
a facsimile reprint
a relatively inexpensive substitute for the real thing
a representative collection
an exact facsimile on vellum
authorized facsimile of the original
careful copies
elegantly reproduced in facsimile
facsimile reproduction in separate mount
fine fascimile, true to the first edition
photographic facsimile on fine paper, taken from a unique copy
reproduced in two colors by the offset process

FANTASY

a fluke of whimsy
appears to be fanciful

contains a number of unusual and rather fanciful items
from the world of imaginary animals
imbued with a lyrical romanticism
romantic rendition of wild scenery
though hypothetical it has a basis in fact
with creatures mythological and monstrous

FAULTS - BORDERS

top border shaved
with a little loss of border

FAULTS - CREASES

bit wrinkled near bottom
crinkled and with damage and crude repair
dim old vertical fold
faint, non-interfering, almost invisible crease
few corners folded
inconspicuous soft crease in the lower right corner
occasional crimping or other slight edge wear
puckered at tips
rippled in a few places
small indent mark
some bending of corners
some rust marks and handling creases
with soft creases visible mostly from the verso
with unintentional foldmarks

FAULTS - DAMAGE

chipped around edges
corner excised
corners bruised
inked underlinings
insect damage limited to one margin
mild cracking throughout
one miniscule nick
single, small stab hole
small hole in background edge

some margins chipped from careless opening
somewhat damaged
the principal defect is...
with an occasional tiny nick
with glue damage to a few letters
with slight loss

FAULTS - DISCOLORING

chaffed with faint browning
clean but mildly browned
evenly faded to brown
faded as usual
gently toned overall
irregular fading
lightly age toned
mildly browned
pale brown mottling
paper uniformly darkened
poor paper used which has yellowed
scattered light scorching
scuffed and partly faded
some fading, principally at extreme lower edge
some time discoloration and old tape
some yellowing of paper
tape shadows on cover and endpapers
the aniline ink is faded
the fugitive colors have faded considerably
time stain and other minor defects
trace of discoloring
trifle darkened on upper half
unobtrusive browning throughout
with gentle patina
with normal pale age toning
with occasional minor blemishing to text

FAULTS - FOLDS

browning at fold and other areas
central crease lightly foxed and tape repaired on verso
has been misfolded
minor separations at folds especially where joined with folder
separations at folds some of which are large but with no loss
short slit at one fold
some creasing along one fold
some fraying at centerfold
some soft creasing along centerfold
some tears at fold junctions
splits along folds with minor loss
weak at central fold
with some loss along fold

FAULTS - FOXING

a few specks of foxing
foxing quite brief
isolated foxing
light to moderate foxing throughout
minor foxing and browning
moderate foxing or offsetting throughout
occasional trifling marginal foxing
scattered foxing yet still a very good copy
sporadic foxing especially on the ends
usually found foxed or stained
variable foxing throughout
with inconsequential faint foxing

FAULTS - MAJOR

an imperfect copy
broken and worn
has had hard use
needing extensive repair
numerous flaws including overall light browning
offered with all faults, without implication of fault
only good at best

only presentable
should be seen
sold as-is
very worn and defective
with a thousand faults
with obvious damage

FAULTS - MARGINS

binding holes in extreme left margin
blank margins chipped and worn, but image fine
dampstain far from image
defects at edges of sheet
edges trimmed close, with some loss of text
few small dampstains, heaviest in margins
foxing in margin barely entering image
marginal flaws can easily be matted out when framed
margins small and chipped
minor marginal darkening
short tears and defects at edges of sheet
shows printers binding holes
side margins appear trimmed but still ample
slightly narrow
small spots of foxing outside the image
some faint spotting in margins and a bit on image
some overall surface dirt, especially evident in blank margins
somewhat frayed but not affecting engraved surface
top margin has a few short splits
trimmed a trifle close
unobtrusive creases near edges of side margins
upper and lower margins trimmed to a quarter of an inch
with brief marginal dampstain
with minor loss in margin

FAULTS - MINOR

a few unimportant age-stains
a little luster lost
a little musty, but clean

burdened with minute flaws
cleanly closed tears
else quite bright and attractive
flawed but charming
looks good, despite its faults
mostly very good
not obtrusive nor to be considered a major flaw
not too noticeable
occasional small loss
showing little wear
somewhat less than fine
straining for very good
unobtrusive little spot
visible but not obtrusive

FAULTS - MISSING PARTS

a corner of the leaf is missing
captions trimmed
issued with... which is lacking in this copy
paper backing partly missing
paper loss in the top right corner
small piece missing
with a jagged triangular chip

FAULTS - OFFSETTING

faint offset lines
mild offsetting
minor browning and offsetting
some offsetting from varnished portion of the transparencies

FAULTS - STAINS, AGE

a few unimportant age stains
edges stained yellow
scattered acidic spots
some dust and time stains
spotted and browned

FAULTS - STAINS, DAMP

dampstaining principally marginal, but affecting some images
mostly marginal dampstaining
partial dampstaining throughout
pinkish damp stain across top extending down two inches
slight marginal dampstaining
time and water stain along the edges

FAULTS - STAINS, MINOR

brief brown spotting
faintest of soiling
imperceptible faint stain
infrequent spots or stains
marginal stain at top which abuts border
minor stains, etc.
occasional spot or other slight blemish
one minor spot, else perfect
small stain mostly on the reverse side
soiling mostly quite minor
spots not too noticable or obtrusive
unobtrusive stain barely entering image
virtually imperceptable stain
with a couple of faint stains

FAULTS - STAINS, SURFACE

a bit of surface soiling in one small area
faintest hint of soiling
few spots and smudges
pale tape stains
small rust spot with tiny hole in it
somewhat soiled but intact
splash staining on lower half
sporadically marked
traces of previous mounting
very light, unobtrusive overall surface soiling
with some mottle
with tape residue

FAULTS - TEARS

a severe tear at one fold
cleanly torn at the fold
only minor tears at edges
several with small tears
short tear enters half-inch into image
small closed tears
small tears, affecting several words
splits mostly pinhole size
trivial tear
unrepaired tear in top
virtually imperceptible closed tear
with unimportant tears

FAULTS - WEAR

a bit bruised
a little waviness of paper
at most shows moderate wear
ends occasionally worn
fair condition only
light scuffing and nicking
little soiled and worn
minor surface dents
moderately scuffed but sound
notorious for turning up tattered
rather rubbed and moderately worn
small abrasion
some fraying to deckle edges
thus a good copy only
torn and frayed
trifle dog-eared
wear at extremities with some chipping
with an occasional rough spot

FAULTS - WORMHOLES

a persistent wormhole
has a couple of microscopic worm holes

marginal worming injuring letters in the running heads
scattered wormholes, mostly marginal
several tiny wormholes though not impairing legibility
some marginal wormtraces
two worm holes, one very small, the other resulting in minor loss

FIRSTS

among the first of its kind
appears here for the first time
contains what may be the earliest reference in print
eventually became the first
first account
first attempt on a grand scale
first obtainable
heretofore not covered
possibly a first time
the first systematic attempt to depict
the first work to deal with...
the much touted debut of...
this is an example of one of the first...

GIFTS

a wonderful and different gift
executed as a gift for...
for any festive occasion
perfect choice
problem solver
specially suited for...

GOOD LOOKING

a decorative item designed for use
a gorgeous presentation
a gracious touch that has all but disappeared
a handsome tribute to...
a striking piece
a stunning display of...
a true spectacle

a very rich effect
a visual gem
a wonderfully decorative piece
a work of art in its own right
a work satisfying to the discriminating eye
an appealing copy
beautiful from all angles
beautifully formed
certainly enhanced by...
delightfully attractive
delighting the eye
esthetically superb
exceptionally pretty
extremely decorative
eye-catching
famous and beautiful
format is both unusual and elegant
handsome to look at
has an air of elegance
highly ornamental
in conservative and elegant taste
in fine appearance
incredibly beautiful
irresistible beauty
looks wonderful
outstanding for its beauty
particularly striking
pleasing uncluttered appearance
precise, well balanced decoration
rare and beautifully designed
rather attractive
should be seen to be properly appreciated
thoroughly handsome
truly pleasing
visually beautiful
will satisfy the discriminating eye
with a fine arts approach to aesthetics

GOOD QUALITY

a reputation for quality work
combines permanence and legibility
for those who appreciate fine craftsmanship
integrates beauty and function
long lasting
of considerable quality
of outstanding quality
technically superior
well designed
will last for centuries
will perform consistently

GOOD VALUE

a good buy
a valuable document
at least as valuable as it is amusing
especially valuable
intrinsically valuable
nothing omitted for the sake of economy
of inestimable value
owes its chief value to...
the universal choice
this will continue to increase in value

HISTORICAL

a retrospective view
a turning point in the history of...
an important link in the chain of events
at a critical historical juncture
documents a forgotten time
important beyond the mere decorative
informative period piece
it is a foundation work in the history of...
marks and elucidates an important phase in the development of...
of considerable historical importance
of major importance in the history of...

one of the most important early works on...
preserves an aspect of our culture
published at a critical time in its history
records many factual details of the way we were
served as the standard for many years
was a strategic document
with considerable historical importance
wonderful historic document

HUMOR

a high comedy view
a highly developed sense of the absurd
a lovely piece of facetiae
comments amusingly
filled with wit and charm
full of mirth
funny and direct
has elegance and humor
imagery is humorous
in many cases most amusing
just as funny today as in the last century
spirited and amusing
the material is presented in an amusing way
this is hilarious

IMPORTANCE

a celebrated work
a cornerstone work
a fine and important work
a masterpiece of its kind
a primary document
a rare and significant contribution
a seminal work
a true classic
a work of the highest authority
an authoritative contribution
an important manifestation

arguably the most important work
exceptionally important
for a long time an authoritative work
immensely interesting and significant
in the top rank
intrinsically important
is significant because...
none is quite as important or sought after as this
of fundamental importance
of special significance
often considered the most crucial
one of, if not the most important
one of the most copied
played an important role
represents the culmination of...
seminal in the creation of...
stands in the front rank of works of its type
the most important and sophisticated
underscoring its importance
unsurpassed in importance

INACCURACIES

a delightful example of the lack of concern for correct images
a distorted picture
a fallacy
a gross distortion of fact
a misnomer
ambiguities abound
an improbable assumption
an over simplification of the true facts
based upon an imperfect knowledge of the facts
bears little resemblance to an actual...
clever but sadly inaccurate remarks
derived from the most inaccurate sources
erroneous conception
given the lack of clarity
his account was taken as genuine

incorrectly states that...
incorrectly portrayed as...
influenced by his preconceived notions
liberally salted with inaccuracies
marred by many inaccuracies
meant to tell the exact truth but
more fantasy than reality
not a scrupulously correct image of the scene
not always scrupulous in providing correct images
notably absent
one wonders how the author came by such information
perpetuating the myth that...
slightly misleading
the evidence does not bear out his claims
will not entirely hold water
with a happy disregard for fact

INCOMPLETE

by no means complete
in an unfinished state
it was never completed

INFLUENCE

exhibits the growing influence of...
gave expression to the change in public taste
generated renewed interest
greatly raised the standards
has a powerful appeal
has influenced succeeding generations
later it would be incorporated into...
made an early and important impact
molded the public's taste for years to come
one of the most influential of all
one of the strongest influences upon...
particularly apt to excite interest
presaged the beginning of...
provoked a great outcry

the first of a new breed
the most influential early attempt
this work established a pattern
was vastly influential

INTENT

especially useful for...
intended for classroom use
intended to attract
meant to appeal to the tastes of the great and wealthy
meant to be useful as well as beautiful
presents an idealized portrait
the intended use was...

INTERESTING

a curious item
affords a fascinating insight
also of interest is...
an added element of interest is provided by...
an immensely interesting work
critically interesting copy
especially salient
interesting and informative
is especially interesting because...
it is interesting to note that
one particularly interesting aspect is...
should interest and provoke
though not one of the rarest, it is one of the most interesting
two features of note are...

MARGINS

crisp and clean with good margins
full sheet printed to the edges
margins trimmed for binding
trimmed but ample

untrimmed with wide margins
with margins averaging two inches
with wide lateral margins

MISTAKES

an understandable miscalculation
either careless or downright fiction
errors and exaggerations are apparent
many errors in the descriptions
this seems to be an error
unintentionally inappropriate

OBSCURITY

little known but wonderful
little known and uncommon
too little known today
was apparently unknown until...

OPINION

given the benefit of the doubt
it is surprising that...
it is now generally accepted that...
it must be assumed that...
it seems highly probable that...
perhaps the most attractive features are...
supposedly was...
the evidence may be thought to indicate otherwise
there can be little question that...
this might possibly be the best
this seems an improbable assumption, but

OPINION - MINE

either... or... I believe the former
first one I have ever seen
has always been a favorite of ours
I believe, and here I'm sticking my neck out
I consider this to be the best and most desirable

I do not have the slightest doubt that...
I hardly think there could be any more beautiful
I highly recommend you buy this one
in my experience this is...
in my judgement
my best guess is
one of my favorites
one of the most attractive I have encountered
one of the nicest we've ever had in stock
original, we believe and judge
our faith in... remains unabated
the first we have encountered
the handsomest we have found thus far
the nicest copy we have handled of this title
this is the first copy I have seen...
to the best of our knowledge and research
we are very partial to...
we believe it to be
we have handled only one other copy
we would surmise that...

OPINION - OTHERS

according to experts
considered by many to be the best...
hailed as revolutionary by...
held in little esteem by...
his own favorite, and considered one of his best by critics
I am told
informed opinion favors the view that...
is considered to be one of his finest
it has been asserted, and generally accepted that...
it is generally considered that...
many experts believe this to be the best
this is considered by many to be the most desireable of all

ORIGINALITY

a novel approach
a work such as this had never been done before
an inclination to depart from the conventional
an unconventional publication
because it is so original
dazzling and original
deliciously different
each one is unique
established a precedent
in a class by itself
in a class of its own
marked by its originality and craftsmanship
opened up a new age
rare, probably unique
sheds new light on...
uniquely blessed

PAPER

a variant printed on thin paper
especially watermarked with...
exhibiting the typical characteristics of handmade stock produced in the middle or late 1830's
foolscap paper, possibly of local manufacture
full-page reproductions on glossy stock paper
illustrations on krome-coat stock
issued on relatively poor quality paper which splits and chips
lettered tissue guards
lightweight with a high opacity
on heavy laid, sized and polished paper
on medium finish paper
on special paper for perfect reproduction
on thin fibrous wove
on watermarked quarto sheets
printed on a fine-textured paper of local manufacture
printed on cream wove paper
the impressed watermark can be clearly seen

treated to prevent further oxidation or degradation
will not discolor or turn brittle with age
wire-lined rag paper
written on paper known to be produced around 1800

PAPER - TYPES

100% rag, acid free, antique, calendered, cast coated, countermarked, esparto, fine art, handmade, linen faced, machine made, matt, medium heavy stock, mouldmade, mourning stationery, pebble finish, ph neutral, rice, twin-wire paper

POPULARITY

a highly acclaimed work
achieved quite a sensational impact
achieved some measure of popularity
acquired a remarkable popularity among...
an instant popular favorite
attracted considerable attention
best known and most impressive
brought the trend to its peak
by popular choice
caused a growing sense of excitement
created a sensation immediately
distributed to a wide public
enjoyed an enormous success
enjoyed great popularity in its time
enormously popular
exceedingly popular and versatile
famous and much sought-after
for the insatiable public appetite
gained wide acceptance from the public
great attention has been paid to...
greatly admired by an enthusiastic audience
highly esteemed
its popularity was due to its attractive design
most beloved of all
much celebrated

obstinately popular among...
one of the most enduring
particularly in demand
perhaps the most desired
publicized by the popular press
quickly became rather famous
served an eager market
something for everyone
the public expressed great enthusiasm for this work
this work gained international renown
very popular in the 19th century
very well known
was highly favored
was very well received from the very beginning
well-known to all
widely disseminated

PRAISE

a dazzling array
a fascinating historical image
a fascinating fabric, rich with detail
a fine presentation which communicates with beauty and power
a magnificent accomplishment
a mine of information
a monumental achievement
a splendid example of...
a state of the art look at...
a striking expression of...
absolutely marvelous
an amazing production
an ambitious work
an engaging contribution to the genre
an inspiring piece
artistically sensitive
becoming a classic
charmingly combines the practical with the picturesque
considered the finest and most decorative

engagingly presented
enlivened by occasional...
fascinating and delightful
fine example of...
finely tuned
has a distinctive look
has considerable charm
has rare insight into...
here's one of those wonderful
it's easy to see why it was awarded...
its charms are difficult to exaggerate
justly regarded as one of the most satisfying
most deserving of attention
not likely to be bettered
of particular merit
one cannot help but be engaged by...
one of the most exciting
particularly complex and desirable
quite extraordinary
richly meaningful
shows restraint
splendid and lavish
the best in a generation
utterly satisfying

PURPOSE

filled a particular local need
for practical use and for decorative purposes
served both as an advertisement and as a source of pride

RARE

a curious item destined for scarcity
a lovely copy of this rarity
a much sought after work
a rare and interesting miscellany
a work of some scarcity
an unbelievable find

certainly very rare today
fascinating and scarce
most unusual
much sought after and often missing or in fascimile
now very rare
of obvious rarity and significance
one of the last from...
one of the rare later examples of...
particularly hard to come by
quite difficult to obtain
rare, especially so complete as here
rare and charming
rare and desirable
rare and fascinating in this form
rarely encountered
scarce in collectible condition
scarce to rare variant of...
traditionally a rarity
undoubtedly scarce thus

RARELY MARKETED

according to auction records, last offered for sale in...
an item that doesn't turn up frequently
first one we've offered in quite some time
has recently become very scarce on the market
no copy has appeared at auction since...
offered for sale only twice in last ten years
seldom available for purchase
seldom offered treasure
very few have come onto the market in modern times

RARER

far more scarce than any other by...
it is far less common than...
probably the rarest of...
rather less common than...
the first and by far the rarer

RAREST

almost unobtainable
apparently the only copy known
as a result of centuries of use few remain
does not survive elsewhere
due to exceeding rarity and great value
early copies are excessively rare
exceptionally scarce
excessively rare in this form
extremely scarce in any condition
fabulously rare
few copies survive; it seems unlikely that more will surface
hardly a dozen survive
has long since disappeared
has never before been publicly offered for sale
it has become nearly impossible to find
its rarity can hardly be overemphasized
nearly unobtainable
never encountered before
no other copy survives, as far as we are aware
notoriously rare
now seems to have vanished
of the greatest rarity
one of only ten copies with hand coloring
only three copies were located according to...
only two other copies known to exist
pieces like this are almost non-existent
regarded as one of the rarest
such examples are rarely found and usually very expensive
the only one produced
ultra scarce
used to turn up occasionally 20 years ago
virtually unobtainable

REPAIRS

evidence of repairs
held in place by paste

light glue stains visible from verso
margins damaged and repaired in several
rejoined where attached at inner margin
remargined on three sides with some glue stains
repaired but broken
somewhat damaged and repaired
with large patch of glue residue

REPAIRS - BACKING

backed with Japanese paper
expertly linen-backed
has been professionally rebacked with modern paper
has been repaired and rebacked
minor repairs and backing
on fine rag paper but laid onto a thin support sheet
rebacked in matching paper

REPAIRS - CLEANING

a cleaned copy
good condition except for remains of previously cleaned foxing
heavily erased
newly restored
several spots where bleach has been used and weakened the paper
washed a long time ago

REPAIRS - EXPERT

a few skillful repairs to minor marginal defects
almost invisibly corrected
apparent skillful restoration
discreetly repaired
expert marginal repair
minor, invisible repair
professionally conserved including deacidification
repaired without loss
some expert restoration

REPAIRS - MARGINS

a few basically insignificant margin repairs on verso
several repaired tears in the margin
slight marginal strengthening
trimmed to side platemarks

REPAIRS - TAPE

acid-free, non-static, reversible document repair tape applied
cello-tape repairs on verso
center fold reinforced from the verso
internally reinforced with paper tape
marginal cellotape repairs in portrait
mended with cloth tape
paper taped across the top margin on verso
reinforced on all sides save one
remains of tape and hinges on verso
remnants of old tape on verso
separated at center fold, tissue laminated
short tear skillfully repaired
shows remnants of old tape
some folds reinforced
tear repaired without surface loss
traces of tape and hinge on verso
two tears restored affecting text but with no loss
with remnant of cloth tape
with short clean tear repaired on verso

SALES PITCH

a good buy
a good number have extra-special features
a perfect companion to...
a pleasure to have and to hold
a sure-fire winner
a true once-in-a-lifetime opportunity
a video-tape of the highlights of the collection is available
a wide variety is available
always in high demand

and as a special bonus
best you can imagine
certain to delight hearts
desirable in every respect
diverse selection
doesn't get much better than this
enhances appreciation and understanding
especially desirable since...
for those who remember
grab this prize
hard to beat
here's a classic for just...
hurry on this one
ideal for display
increase your enjoyment year after year
not to be missed
obviously very desirable
on the cutting edge
our exclusive
owning this makes for great historic entertainment
perfect to hand down through the generations
quite a treasure trove
something extra special
special selection
the best deal ever offered
there is an obvious market for this
this is the real thing
this should sell fast
we are pleased to offer
we are pleased to announce the availability for purchase
we'll throw in...
well worth a look
will enhance your appreciation of...
will please you
you'll like this piece
you'll love seeing this one

SIZE - LARGER

big, bright and beautiful
conspicuously oversized
extravagantly large
gigantic
huge
imposing size
large, unwieldy sheet
mammoth
massive
of heroic proportions
on a full sheet
on a generous scale
rather monumental
somewhat larger format
twice as large as usual
very large and imposing
very prominent

SIZE - SMALLER

a lovely miniature in fresh condition
an unusually small...
charming miniature
copied in reduced form
designed to take little space
diminutive and irresistibly attractive
due to space limitations
dwarfed by...
given the lack of size
narrow
smaller but more decorative
thin
various small sizes
very slight

SOURCE

a combination of first hand experience and reports from local informants
based on the information from...
based on the superb collection of...
based on the originals
borrowed from...
compiled from...
consistent with a Spanish origin
derived from...
exclusive source
first appearing in...
first published in...
from a very important work which documents...
from an early overland journal
from the unique copy in...
has leaned heavily on...
originally issued by...
primarily American in origin
recently imported from...
shows the same essential information as appeared on the original
source no doubt, is one of the later editions of...
the result of careful examination
these are from the rarer edition
was largely drawn from...
with the compliments of...

SOURCE - UNCERTAIN

from an unidentified edition
it is difficult to pinpoint the exact source of...
one may look askance at his sources
the source is conjectural, but likely...
unsure of exact source

STYLE

air of pastoral serenity
delicate and light feeling

emphasizes line and design
in a style reminiscent of a much earlier period
in the grand manner
opted for simplicity
reflects his personal style
sturdiness and function came before decoration
the most restrained simplicity of form
utilitarian, lean design
with graceful, curving lines

SUCCESS

a brilliant success
a considerable success
achieved a standard that equalled or surpassed its time
an unqualified success at the time
few have been so completely successful
highly successful
succeeded beyond all expectations

SUPERLATIVES

a superb specimen
a superior copy in all respects
a superlative work
considered the finest
considered to be the most decorative
here is the best of its kind
its uniqueness lies in...
most effective
most impressive
most luxurious
not likely to be surpassed
on an equal plane with the best
one of the most famous cases of...
one of the greatest of all time
one of the three best
one of the best and most versatile
one of the most appealing

quite superior
splendid, lavish, and monumental
superb example of...
the best available
the epitome of...
the finest ever to appear
the finest of all which have surfaced in the past
the most celebrated and the most influential
the ultimate
this is doubtless the finest copy extant
thought by many to be the finest available
top quality
without qualification it is one of the best

TIME - EARLY

a particularly early and attractive example of...
a relic of our national infancy
a very early look at...
an extremely early document
certainly one of the earliest printings in miniature format
earlier and dramatically different
from its beginning
from one of the earliest
from the beginning of the previous century
had strong beginnings
it appears to be one of the earliest accounts
one of the earliest appearances
provides one of the few early sketches
reflects some of the excitement of the early days
revolutionary for its time
the earliest extant edition dates from...
the starting point

TIME - PERIOD

a bit of nineteenth century curiosa
a comprehensive modern treatment
a period of exuberant growth

as it appeared at a single point in time
at the transitional stage
by now well established
covers the war years
for its time
gives an intimate view of the eighteenth century
golden age
in the period of western expansion
in the tradition of the eighteenth century
late in the colonial period
mindful of its place in time
provides us with a precious snapshot of these locations at the time
related to today
some time ago
sometime after...
the period of supremacy of...
when urbanization was well on its way

TIME - SPAN

a decade of economic and political unrest
a hiatus of three years
a richly diverse past and present
almost continuously through the 18th century
ancient and modern
authoritative through the nineteenth century
covers a wide range of topics from the sixteenth century on
in the intervening years
over a span of fifty years
over the course of five centuries
the period from 18.. to 19.. was a crucial one
the source of inspiration for several centuries
through years of transition
throughout the ages
throughout much of the era
throughout the ante-bellum decade

UNCERTAINTIES

apparently definitive
contemporary information is lacking
I assume this is... but I can find no information on it
it is distinctly possible that...
it may be important to say...
less well known to us
one puzzling feature is...
some confusion might arise as to priority
this may or may not be original but does not survive in other copies
unknown at this time
unknown to us
was at first believed to be
we have been unable to determine if...

UNCOMMON

achieved a degree of sophistication rarely encountered
all variants are uncommon
almost as scarce as the first issue
an uncommon version
an unusual depiction of...
becoming rare
curious and rather intriguing
decidedly uncommon
declining number available
exotic rendering
from the famous... and getting scarce...
hard to find
increasingly difficult to locate
not exactly rare, but not encountered every day
not particularly easy to come by
presumably uncommon
scarcely a vestige remains
simple but unusual
something of a curiosity
uncommon in this format
uniquely blessed

UNCONVINCING

doubt was cast on his findings
hard to believe
his objectivity is questionable at best
more style than substance
presenting an idealized portrait
presents groundless theories
rambling and generally unconvincing
there is a lack of empirical evidence to support...
unsupported by research

UNORIGINAL

basically identical to...
bears a faked signature of...
bears a striking resemblance to...
borrowed without acknowlegement
extremely skillful pen-and-ink facsimile on similar paper
intended to emulate the success of...
no better or worse but typical of the period
nonoriginal
offers nothing original since it is based on previously printed sources
slightly conventional flavor
supplied in facsimile
virtually indistinguishable from

UNPUBLISHED

a third volume, although called for, was never published
apparently unpublished
commissioned but never published
never published in its entirety
no copies were produced for sale

WANTS

actively buying
advise us of what you have
all types wanted
always buying rare and desireable items

always interested in fine single items or entire collections
avidly seeking desirable copies
buying, selling, swapping
buying collections or single items
buying in all fields
cash for...
collections wanted
desperately seeking
eagerly looking for...
highest prices paid
I buy anything related to...
I purchase accumulations
I will pay for the following
I'm always seeking replacement stock
I'm interested in purchasing
if you are selling I want to buy
include price with quote
no collection too large or too small
paying $100 for...
permanent want, please save
permanently required
please offer at all times
please quote anything, anytime
please quote any quantity
please write or call
primary want
related items wanted
seeking worthwhile items
send all relevant catalogs
send for our permanent want list
urgently needed
want lists are most welcome
wanted please quote
we are always interested in buying
we are purchasing and selling

we deal exclusively in...
we invite your offers
will travel to purchase

WORTHWHILE

a truly impressive production
a worthy speciman
an accomplished work
an especially valuable work
an essential work
destined to become indispensable
eminently significant
especially noteworthy
generally excellent
inspires awe
most deserving of attention
possessing much merit
takes on new significance
truly worthwhile
valuable for exhibiting a view of...

Books

ADVERTISEMENTS

a profusion of advertisement leaves
advertising matter is as called for in BAL
an abundance of ads at the end
complete with two leaves of ads at the back
mainly promotional but with great ads
with boxed ad at front
with several ads at the rear
with two pages of terminal ads

ANTHOLOGY

a collection of columns from...
a compilation of papers
a coordinated treasury on all aspects of...
a cornucopia of superb articles and stories
a daft and dizzy collection
a dozen fine writers have come together to create a memorable portrait
a quirky, moody, funny assembly of pieces
also contains work by...
comprises much of the best writing of...
culled from works published since...
important literary assemblage
includes a few poems never before published
includes one story not in any other anthology
includes part of our literary heritage
incorporates the best material from several earlier works
never before anthologized
prominently featured are the works of...
selections from this richly textured body of work
the definitive collection of...
with contributions by several correspondents from the war

ANTHOLOGY - PRAISE

a charming collection of...
a delightful nostalgic collection of...
an enchanting selection of short stories
an inviting and insightful anthology
an outstanding assemblage showcasing the work of...
delightful collection of tales
written by an authoritative group of experts

ASSOCIATION COPY

author's own copy, with his signature and date
recipient was a friend of the author's
this copy was read by...

ASSOCIATION COPY - PRAISE

a first-rate association copy
a superb association copy of a scarce book
an association copy of the highest order
an extraordinarily significant association copy
an important association copy

AUTOBIOGRAPHY

a direct and personal record
a minutely detailed diary
a self-interview addressing pertinent questions
a story of the personal experience of...
an autobiographical saga
anecdotes of personal experience
based on his personal observations
contains details of the author's escapades
the genuine memoirs of...

AUTOBIOGRAPHY - PRAISE

a splendid autobiography by one of the mainstays of...
a vivid first hand account
an extraordinary memoir

AUTOGRAPHS - AUTHOR

a couple of corrections are made in holograph
a good large example of the author's hand
a number of revisions and deletions in author's hand
accompanied by the author's typescript, with autograph corrections
added by the author at a later point using a different pen
contains substantive holographic corrections in author's hand
correction in author's hand on page ten
cut signature of author laid in
early signature of the author on free endpaper
initialled by the author at the conclusion
occasional ink diagrams in his hand
small ink corrections, presumably by the author
the author's notations are extensive and amusing
with a holograph colophon written in the author's hand
with a passage from the book copied out in the author's hand
with an ink correction in the author's hand
with his holograph note tipped in

AUTOGRAPHS - MULTIPLE

a desirable assemblage of signatures
additionally signed by the other poets at their contributions
copies with signatures of author and illustrator are rare
signed by each poet at his or her contributions
signed by several of the artists represented in the volume

AUTOGRAPHS - RARE

difficult title to locate inscribed
examples of his handwriting are of the utmost rarity
with the seldom found signature

AUTOGRAPHS - STYLE

boldly signed
clean, legible signature
faint eighteenth-century signature
signature is legible and of reasonable dimensions
with his characteristically large signature

written in a humanistic hand
written in a seventeenth-century hand
written in an open letter script
written in disciplined cursive script

BINDER

a handsome copy of this binding designed by...
a scarce piece by this book designer
became the most important binder of his time
binding is said to have been designed by...
brown morocco blind tooled by...
fine circular binder's ticket of...
from the Mearne bindery
produced some of the finest bindings ever conceived
the binding is probably one of the earliest produced by...
the most elaborate binding by the ... binder so far recorded
with the binder's ticket on endpaper
with the spine imprint of...

BINDING - CLOTH

brocade covered boards
embossed cloth
green institutional buckram
original pictorial cloth
original rough linen binding
silk cloth over flexible boards

BINDING COPY

a prime candidate for rebinding
a taken-down copy ready for rebinding
internally perfect, ideal for rebinding
sold as a binding copy not subject to return
the book has been pulled but needs re-binding

BINDING DECORATIVE

blind-tooled roll borders
both covers similarly decorated

comfortable as well as ornamental
covers panelled in blind and with large arabesque centerpiece
covers with large strapwork panel composed of onlays
decorated paper over flexible boards
decoration is similar to the original binding on...
decoratively stamped cloth
dense foliate tooling
emblematically tooled
embossed cover medallion
glazed boards
in a cameo binding
in a fanfare binding
in the emblematical binding
large central lozenge
oval inset on the front
parchment-backed marbled boards
turn-ins elaborately decorated
two-toned boards
with arabesque pattern in center
with circular albumen print inset to front cover

BINDING - ECONOMICAL

a clean, sturdy, but not expertly accomplished binding
a plain and unassuming binding
a rare wartime production
an economically made wartime book
an inexpensively produced book
buckram backed boards
cloth-backed boards
covers decorated in oriental leaf
in a less expensive octavo format
in a remainder binding
in a serviceable binding
in an inexpensive basil binding
in very good condition for this cheapest of productions
inexpensive but well produced
inexpensive production in inexpensive binding

issued at a modest price
modern library buckram
old full leather rebacked with utilitarian buckram
purely utilitarian
simply bound
sound and serviceable
spiral bound
stamped in discolored dutch leaf
stolidly useful and satisfactory
the binding is a model of simplicity and sobriety
the less desirable colonial binding

BINDING - EXHIBITION

a one-of-a-kind exhibition binding
an elaborate table book
an example of durability and artistic presentation
lovely exhibition binding
most likely an exhibition binding
one of the most important examples of the design work of...
will delight connoisseurs of fine bookbinding

BINDING - GILT

all over gold tooled
broad gilt border of connected fleurs-de-lis
densely gilt-stamped leather
elaborately tooled with gilt geometric designs
exquisitely adorned with palladium and gold
gilt and blind panelled
gilt and gauffered edges
gilt dentelles
gilt dog-tooth border
handsomely gilt with wide floral and ornamental border
intricately stamped in gilt
ribbed in six gilt-ruled panels
tooled with arabesque designs in gilt
triple gilt fillet bordered cover
with single gilt-ruled border on covers

BINDING - LABEL

color pictorial cover label
expertly rebacked with paper spine label nicely restored
gilt-lettered morocco backstrip labels
hand-lettered label and spine
later paper spine labels added
morocco label in spine compartment
printed paper labels
with paper spine label nicely restored

BINDING - LEATHER

crushed morocco
full leather tooled in blind
full straight grain morocco
gilt-lettered vellum with silk ties
gilt-ornamented and lettered leather
half-morocco, incorporating pictorial portions of wrappers
hard-grained morocco
limp suede spine and corners
modern mottled calf
modern Spanish polished speckled calf
original reversed cowhide
publisher's black leather gilt
sheep-backed boards
vellum stamped in black
with inlaid morocco designs
with leather joints

BINDING - METAL PARTS

brass catches
covers with large pierced brass corner pieces
original silver clasps and catches
ornamental metal cornerpieces on both covers
silver upper cover with symbolic ornaments
with the remains of two clasps

BINDING - ONLAYS

elaborately hand-tooled with onlaid coloured roses
enhanced by numerous leather onlays
large panels of onlaid black morocco
original blue cloth with mounted cover photograph
pictorial cover applique
with an onlaid silhouette
with an onlaid hand-painted portrait on ivory
with an onlay in coloured leathers on the front
with modelled onlays in sunken panels on the front

BINDING - OTHER MATERIAL

bound in linson
felt over boards
in a pressboard pamphlet binder
linen-backed leatherette
original simulated leather
with integral cover

BINDING - PERIOD

19th century tooled calf
chapbook
early vellum
gilt polished calf in period style
in an attractive period binding
modern sheep, antique style
seventeenth-century speckled calf
turn-of-the-century full green morocco

BINDING - PICTORIAL

an unusual, well-detailed pictorial binding
in original pictorial laminated boards
pictorial cloth designed by...

BINDING - PRAISE

a bold and dramatic binding
an impressive, stately binding

appealing for the survival of its printed boards
beautifully hand tooled
book design harmonious with contents
bound in the most craftsmanlike way
encased in beauty
immaculately and very finely bound
in a sparkling binding
in a spectacular binding
in a sumptuous binding
in handsome gilt lettered covers
sturdily bound
the signet is present and in perfect condition

BINDING REPAIRS - COVER

blank lower cover possibly supplied
corners renewed
expertly recased
later cloth with original paper wrappers bound-in
neatly recornered
new half calf over contemporary marbled boards
original cloth covers and spine bound in rear of each volume
rebacked with leather similar to the original
recently rebound in undyed sheepskin
reset in binding
sympathetically rebacked in compatible cloth

BINDING REPAIRS - HINGES AND JOINTS

carefully strengthened at hinges
hinge and a few gutters tape-strengthened
hinges archivally reinforced
hinges tightened at an early date
joints crudely strengthened
strengthened at inner margin

BINDING REPAIRS - SPINE

carefully rebacked preserving original spine
ends of spine expertly renewed

ingeniously rebound, saving spine
rebacked with original spine laid down
spine chipped with contemporary repairs
spine corroded and partially rebacked with binder's tape
spine covering attached with tape to covers
spine crudely taped
spine laid down on newer parchment
with a neat internal mend at crown of spine
with recently taped spine

BINDING - SEWN

a strange production, stitched at the top
hand sewn headbands
newly stitched
spine restitched by hand

BINDING - SPECIAL

a specially bound copy
an extra bound edition of...
books are uniformly bound, possibly for the author
in a beautiful custom binding
in a personalized binding
in an exquisite signed binding
in the presentation binding
one of very few extant in this binding
this format is extremely unusual
unusual to find a copy in such an attractive binding

BINDING - SPINE

bound with a flat back
decorative backstrip
floral motif in backstrip compartments
ribbed gilt-decorated spines
spine in ornate gold with raised bands
spine with double raised bands
with false bands

BINDING - STYLE

a composite book, consisting of...
a lovely Art Nouveau binding
also present is the wrap-around band which reads...
board edges bevelled
bound dos-a-dos
bound with divinity circuit edges
clearly an Italian binding
contemporary English mosaic binding
gilt-ruled turn-ins
in a counterfeit Aldine binding
in a tight back binding
in cottage-style binding
in the secondary binding
lower cover continues to form flap over upper cover
old limp vellum
original color and gilt lithographed boards
slightly flexible boards
the hard-bound version
this book turns up in three different bindings
wallet edged binding
with a flexible binding
with chamfered edges
with flush boards
with laced-on boards
with tasselled tie
yapp edges

BINDING - TITLE

flat spine decoratively gilt with title in seven compartments
gilt title stamped on front
hand-painted title on spine
the title appears in an enclosed square
title in morocco spine label
typographic cover design

BINDING - WRAPS

bradbound printed wrappers
disbound with decorated wrappers added
embossed lettered wrappers
French marbled wraps
modern marbled wrappers
original wrappers bound into later protective covers
particularly rare in the original wrappers
plain self-paper wrappers
printed wrapper over plain wrapper
punched and string-tied in wrappers
self-paper wrappers, cord-tied
some wrappers missing or tape-repaired
stiff pictorial wraps
text gatherings and plates unbound in wrappers as issued
there was no hard cover edition
trial state of front wrapper laid in
unsewn in original wrappers
white paper used as protective wrapper

BIOGRAPHY

a disguised biography
a literary biography
a look at the childhood and early years of...
a minute biography
a study of his life through his own words and work
an intimate portrait of...
contains details of his domestic life
contains much biographical data on...
contains selections from his correspondence
details of his life are somewhat sketchy
discusses his public and his private life
essentially an account of his life
gave a brief characterization of...
his own story
includes reminiscences of...
including the life and correspondence of...

largely drawn from his correspondence
many details of his life can be found here
personal glimpses of...
pictorial study of a life
profiles the career and contributions of...
tells of his joys and satisfactions
this study examines his work
with a genealogical analysis of the family
with comments on many personal matters

BIOGRAPHY - PRAISE

a candid biography
a great new biography
a wealth of biographical information
an excellent account of the life and work of...
considered the most authoritative biography
important work on his career
interesting for its biographical details
much of biographical interest
the first totally convincing portrait
the funniest sports biography written
this reminiscence is a fascinating portrait

BOOKPLATES

armorial bookplate
bookplate has left slight offset on the inscription opposite
bookplate in folding case
bookplate of noted collector
bookplate unobtrusively removed
dedication copy, with bookplate of the dedicatee
eighteenth-century bookplate
made more valuable by the addition of this bookplate
offset from leather booklabel
small bookplate under dust jacket flap
special bookplate indicating this copy was made especially for...

BOOKPLATES - PRAISE

attractive leather booklabel
with a neat and stylish bookplate
with a tasteful bookplate
with his distinctive pictorial bookplate

BREAKER

breaking copy
in sheets of this scarce book
offered for plates only
seriously defective
sold as a collection of plates not subject to return

CANCELS

cancel slip pasted over...
from the English sheets with the new title-leaf a cancel
half-title is a cancel
in the rare uncancelled state
leaf cancelled as in all known copies
misprints cancelled by pasting correction slips on top
with the inserted unnumbered leaf

CENSORED

in its time it was widely rejected
one of the most famous of "banned books"
printed in Europe, as no American publisher would risk it
the furor that attended publication extends to this day
the text must have been drastically expurgated
this original edition was immediately suppressed
this work was long-suppressed

CHAPTERS

a very helpful chapter for the beginner includes...
an inexpensive edition with run on chapters
contains chapters on all aspects of...
devotes a large segment to an account of...
has a fifteen page chapter devoted to...

the entire chapter is devoted to...
the final chapter is given over completely to...
the final section discusses...
the introductory first part deals with...
there is even a chapter on...
with epigraphs rather than chapter titles
with epigraphs rather than chapter heads

COLLATION

first and last leaves are conjugate, forming a wrap-around
in quires of six leaves
inspected, collated, and restored by...
this example combines elements of both the first and second printings in its collation
with a register given on the colophon page
with page 43 as a singleton
with turned chain-lines

COLLATION BLANKS

lacking the terminal blank
with blank leaves for the addition of portraits,etc.
without initial blank

COLLATION - COMPLETE

all preliminary leaves present
collated and complete
complete with a preliminary errata leaf
final errata leaf present
probably complete, but not collated
with the title and dedication leaves inserted as conjugates

COLLATION - EXTRA

has an additional leaf not mentioned in...
this copy has two extra leaves to the normal edition

COLLATION - SOPHISTICATED

a made-up copy, with ... inserted from another copy
photographs of missing pages supplied
several other leaves possibly supplied
sophisticated but attractive copy
with four pages supplied in photocopy
with two leaves evidently inserted from another copy

COMPARTMENTS

a pocket in the front of the book holds...
leaves cut and hollowed out to form a concealed compartment
lower cover has a compartment which holds...

CONDITION - GOOD

a fresh entirely unsophisticated copy
a fresh unpressed copy
a stunning copy of this great book
a superb copy inside and out
a superior copy of this title
a very fine copy with remnants of the original mailing box
a very good untrimmed copy
bright and clean with hinges intact
clean and fresh internally
contents clean, crisp, and tight
cords intact
fine and fresh inside and out
fine with wrapabout band intact
generally sound
has benefitted from careful and loving ownership
internally crisp and wholly untrimmed
overall sound and presentable
quite tight and fresh
tightly bound
unmarked internally
very good to fine throughout

CONDITION - GOOD UNCOMMON

a nice copy of a work which is prone to wear due to its size
a wartime book difficult to locate in acceptable condition
increasingly scarce in nice condition
never an easy book to obtain, especially in acceptable condition
this binding is a sturdy survivor
usually found in lamentable condition

CONTENT

a cheerful piece of erotica
a detailed overview
a full exposition
a view of the political conduct of...
a wide-ranging contemplation
an anecdotal record
chiefly deals with...
comprised of extensive discussions
contains a plain statement of...
contains vital information concerning...
covers such central facets of the subject as...
directly related to...
discusses topics as varied as...
entirely devoted to a description of...
focusing largely on...
gives us the details regarding...
has some quite telling remarks about...
it treats of...
other items of note include...
over twenty pages of his book are consigned just to...
references both explicit and implicit are made to...
shows examples of...
the document reads in part...
the physical format of the book reflects the importance of the contents
the text includes references to...

CONTENT - BETTER

a wealth of new information
contains many worthwhile observations on...
has more information than usual
he has filled its pages with a wealth of authentic detail
it is most unusual in that it contains ...
often regarded as the best work on...
the conclusions here shed new light on...
the first full-scale examination of the inner workings of...
uniquely combines... with...

CONTENT - PRAISE

a challenging collection of thoughtful concepts
a concise synopsis
a mine of first-hand Americana
a most provocative book
a remarkable insight into the world of...
an eye-opening survey of...
an impartial study for anyone with an interest in...
an impressively detailed survey of...
contains much else of interest
in one of the books best moments...
offers fresh insight and new revelations
peppered with stunning paradoxes
provides a valuable glimpse into the creative process
the subject has spawned an impressive body of literature
well annotated and with full descriptions
with ebullient remarks
with illuminating comments

CONTROVERSY

a persuasive argument for their side
a thorough book that explores both sides of the issue
an examination of the various charges against...
arguably one of the most controversial credos ever written
aroused speculation regarding his intentions
calm and dispassionate vindication of...

carried a seed of controversy
charge and countercharge in the controversy concerning...
forever attracting new questions
his most controversial work to date
his views, though unquestionably right, were unpopular
includes important arguments concerning...
indisputable evidence supports his theory
is quite vehement about...
it provoked a great outcry
offers more conclusive evidence than...
ought to spark debate
provoking and controversial
the bitter ideological enemy of...
the political implications are obvious
the publication of this book led to a rift between...
written with a cheerful indifference to public opinion

CRITICIZES

a critical look at the work of...
a harshly critical but well-documented account of...
a manifesto against...
a reply to...
a revolutionary fusilade
a scathing expression of contempt
an incendiary attack on...
it attacks the credibility of...
meanspirited and gratuitous attack on...
prepared a forceful argument against...
provides a critical analysis of ...'s writings
questions the validity of...
raises provocative questions about...
remonstrance against...
the text is severely critical of...

CRITICISM

a disparaging essay on...
a distinctly dull diatribe

a series of facile predictions
a vitriolic lambasting of liberal politics
an example of the poet's labored prose
an imperfect look at...
contemptuous of the reader
contrary to what the title would have you believe
filled with provincialisms and slang
he wanders fitfully through his subject matter
his stilted prose brings the characters to death
in it, he fulminates against...
invective against...
it does not enlist the reader's sympathy
makes a simple subject complex
oblique rather than straightforward in its approach
rootless and drifting
technically unskilled

CRITICIZED

the account sometimes rambles
the arguments are fatuous
the tone is self-congratulatory
with long and irritating footnotes
a lengthy public response to criticism aroused by...
savagely reviewed
the book was greeted with ridicule and contempt

DUST JACKET - ART

dust jacket art was risque for the times
exceptionally bright pictorial dust jacket
graced by a graphic illustration
in spectacular pictorial dust jacket

DUST JACKET - ARTIST

color covers and other illustrations by...
cover art was executed by...
executed the dust wrapper design
his dust jackets are especially recognizable

in dust jacket illustrated with a painting by...
jacket is designed and illustrated by...
with jacket illustration by the author

DUST JACKET - GOOD CONDITION

an exceptionally nice example of this dust jacket
rarely encountered in such a pristine jacket
the jacket has none of the usual spine fade

DUST JACKET - PARTIAL

dust jacket missing most of the spine portion
in defective but largely complete dust jacket
in dust jacket lacking most of spine
portions of original dust jacket laid in
with front of dust jacket laid in

DUST JACKET - RARE

a rare early dust jacket
often erroneously catalogued as having been issued without a dust jacket
scarce in the tissue jacket
with the uncommon dust jacket

DUST JACKET - REPAIRS

dust jacket expertly repaired at front spine fold
endflaps affixed with tape
neatly, but unnecessarily, reinforced jacket

DUST JACKET - SIZE

in a slightly oversized dust jacket
jacket is full size to match height of book
jacket slightly undersized, as issued

DUST JACKET - STYLE

in original unprinted dust jacket
rear panel features...

with biographical blurb on rear flap
with blurbs by...
wrap-around protective cover

DUST JACKET - TYPE

dust jacket plasticized
glassine jacket with printed paper flaps
in decorated glossy stiff paper wrappers
in foil dust jacket
in fragile rice paper dust jacket
in original printed acetate dust jacket
in publisher's clear plastic jacket
in unprinted white tissue jacket
paper-over-fabric dust jacket
wrapped in proof dust jacket

EARLY MANUSCRIPTS - DECORATIVE

capitals rubricated
colophon on last page within decorative penwork cartouche
demonstrates a free and graceful style of ornamentation
embellished with elegant and dextrous figures
historiated initials throughout
in lower margin is a medieval flourished banderole with motto
initial letters executed in red
knotwork with lacertine convolution and extremities
neatly ruled in columns
opening letters of each line touched in yellow
ruled in very faint plummet
scroll work filled in with light blue and green
very ornamental line fillers throughout
with entrelac intitals

EARLY MANUSCRIPTS - HANDWRITTEN

an early manuscript in Court hand
each part handwritten by a different scribe
florid pen work
headline supplied in a later hand, otherwise unrubricated

in a monastic hand
ornamental letters with free strokes and flourishes of pen
sidenotes in several microscopic hands
small natural fault in vellum avoided by scribe
some medieval nota marks
the medieval sidenotes are in several extremely small hands
with a faint sketch on the dorse
with round open lettering
written in a fine Gothic hand
written in dark brown ink in a microscopic gothic bookhand

EARLY MANUSCRIPTS - ILLUMINATED

floriated wood-engraved initials
heightened with white tracery on burnished gold grounds
illuminated initials with marginal extensions
illustrations and decorations heightened with silver and gold
pictorial woodcut initials
richly adorned with gold lettering
rubricated in red and blue
spaces for initial capitals, some with guide letters
the pictorial initials are four lines high
with an illuminated inscription
written in perfectly formed rustic capitals

EARLY MANUSCRIPTS - PRAISE

a sumptuously illustrated bestiary
a superb example of Coptic manuscript decoration

EARLY MANUSCRIPTS - REPAIRS

a few margins with medieval repairs
several lines strengthened with ink

EDGES

all edges gilt
all edges marbled
concealed beneath the gold of the fore-edge is a scene
deckle edges darkened by dust

fore and bottom edges uncut
gauffered with an elaborate pattern
gilt over untrimmed edges
red sprinkled edges
top edges silver
with a double fore-edge painting
with all edges chased
with all edges burnished
with fore-edge painting of a London view
with fore-edge gauffered
with printed edges
with thumb tab index

EDITION - ABRIDGED

an abridgement of the first edition
extracted from...
faithfully abridged from...
footnotes were largely omitted in this edition
mostly in reduced format
reduced version

EDITION - BETTER

a grand edition
a rare case where the second edition is of more value than the first
best edition, revised and expanded
better and rarer than the first edition
better printed than the first edition and thus still desirable
first and best of several editions
has several inferior reprints
improved edition
not the first, but the preferred edition
second and best edition
the definitive edition
the finest of all editions to bear this imprint
the most highly sought-after version
there are several inferior reprints of this edition
this edition is to be preferred

EDITION - CORRECTED

a corrected and improved edition
a new edition corrected
diligently corrected
issue with errata partly corrected
reissue with additions and corrections
reissued with emendations
reprint with a few corrections
with corrigenda on final leaf

EDITION - DELUXE

a new and elegant edition
deluxe edition with superior quality plates
large paper issue
one of 75 copies on rag paper
one of only six copies printed on vellum
one of the copies printed on better paper
one of the rare copies specially printed on...
produced by hand, utilizing only handmade materials
an unusual item of early printing

EDITION - EARLY

as early an edition as one is likely to find
essentially the earliest procurable edition
first complete edition in book form
first edition thus
first edition in wraps (issued simultaneously with clothbound)
first genuine octavo edition
first regularly published book, preceded by a few rare pamphlets
first separately published
it is the editio princeps of...
most extensive early work on...
no earlier copy is known to survive
only a few copies printed before
precedes the limited edition
preserves an earlier state of the colophon
published before the official account

simultaneous with the first edition
the basis of later editions
the first extant edition
there seems little doubt that this version is the earlier
there were a number of printings but this is the earliest
there were at least six subsequent printings

EDITION - ENLARGED

a more extensive version
an expansion of his earlier work
augmented edition
contains some material not present in the earlier editions
expanded including a new collection
greatly augmented and expanded
heavily revised, with extensive additions
issued in conjunction with...
new edition, with a supplement
revised and enlarged over the limited edition
somewhat expanded from the first edition
the text was reprinted several times, with accretions
the variorum editon of...
this edition includes for the first time...
to this has been added two previously published articles
which appeared in a truncated version as...
with a supplement added
with countless additions and revisions
with several plates not in the first edition

EDITION - FIRST

a paperback original
additional printings not indicated
elusive first issue
first and only edition of...
first edition of the author's first book
first edition of one of the rarest titles on this subject
first edition, first issue
first edition of this separate supplement

hitherto unavailable in book form
it is now plain that this edition takes precedence
modern first edition
of unquestionable priority
the earliest printed version
the first book to bear the imprint of...
there is no statement of edition in the true first printing

EDITION - ILLUSTRATED

a superbly illustrated edition
an emblem book of late 16th century
an excellent edition with many plates
enhanced with extra illustrations
includes numerous leaves of plates
the first well-illustrated edition

EDITION - LATER

a later issue of the first trade edition
a new impression printed from standing type
a re-impression
a reprint, but very nice
all the earlier editions are very scarce
an early recension
appeared with some regularity
facsimile reprint
first American edition, printed in London the year before
first appearance in octavo format
first collective edition
first combined printing of this work previously in two volumes
first public edition, following a subscriber's limited edition
first published on the continent earlier the same year
first unillustrated appearance
follows the first edition closely
in the same format as the first
last lifetime edition
never before published in the U.S.
new editions appeared at frequent intervals

preceded by two editions
replicates the first U.S. edition
stapled offprints
the last edition to bear his name
the pirated English edition
there were a number of editions of this work
third edition (but not so stated)
third in series
unchanged edition

EDITION - LIMITED

a one-of-a-kind production
also printed in other limitations
an unnumbered presentation copy
autographed edition
experience suggests a larger edition was printed than the limitation purports
issued in a small edition
one of...copies (with numerous subvariants)
printed in an edition reputed to have been limited to...
rare limited collector's edition
the only signed limited edition
this copy not numbered

EDITION - NUMBERED

edition of twenty-five
hand-numbered edition
limited to fifty copies, this one out-of-series
number six of an unspecified limited edition
one of 45 copies bound thus
one of only 100 numbered copies on Japanese vellum

EDITION - RARE

a rare and beautifully designed edition
a rare and unique edition
a rare pirated edition

the American edition is more scarce than the English, even this side of the Atlantic
the earliest in private hands
the hardbound version of this is harder to find
the scarce edition printed at...
uncommon, as this edition was intended for limited circulation

EDITION - RETITLED

first edition under this title
published in the U.S.A. under the title...
reissue with new title-page and cover
second edition (with altered title)
subsequent editions were issued under different titles
this work also appeared with the title...

EDITION - REVISED

a landmark reinterpretation
a supplement was issued
completely different in size and appearance from the trade edition
first American edition, with many differences from the English
had considerable revisions made after the first printing
identical to the trade edition with the following exceptions:
incorporates part of the earlier edition
newly updated masterpiece
not the direct equivalent of any single earlier edition
previously published as...
printed in 10 point type rather than the 12 of the earlier edition
reissued and/or revised
reissued in this format as a companion volume to...
reprint, with rearrangements, of the second edition
revised edition containing several intercalary poems not in...
successive editors destroyed the flavor of the original version
this book contains some alterations
this edition prints... for the first time
virtually a new work
with significant variations from the earlier edition
with some changes

EDITION - SECOND

apparently a re-issue of the first edition
first American edition with these illustrations
preceded only by...
reprint of the rare first edition
second and last issue
second impression
second run
the important second edition of a classic
there is thought to be one earlier edition
this edition was apparently preceded by another

EDITION - SPECIAL

a keepsake produced for...
a large-print edition
a lovely press book
a modern fine press edition
a repaginated offprint from the periodical
a school edition
a solid-dot Braille edition
an offprint from an anthology
an unauthorized edition printed by...
an unrecorded printing
an unusual edition
apparently unique, specially printed for...
book was issued in two formats
collotype reproduction of...
his works were printed for private use of...
no comparable edition published
special presentation issue with specially printed endpaper
this edition failed to meet with the author's approval

EDITION - SUBSCRIBER'S

an example of the scarce subscriber's editions issued by...
no limitation given but subscribers are listed
originally sold only to subscribers
printed for subscribers only

EDITION - TIME PERIOD

a 19th-century reprint of the 18th-century original edition
conjecturally dated...
first published in 1920 without illustrations
in the 1900 edition of the same title
most complete edition issued during author's lifetime
one of several editions that year
posthumous printing
published at various dates from... to...
published the same year as the original edition
published to commemorate the author's birthday
re-issued after a gap of more than twenty years
the last edition published in the author's lifetime

EDITION - UNCERTAIN

actual date of publication is unknown
amidst a flurry of competing editions, priority is difficult to establish
an apparently unrecorded issue
has the unrecorded imprint of...
I can find no reference to this production
in the scarcer of two bindings (priority not determined)
it seems likely that this printing was primary
likely the first edition
may have been issued separately
may possibly have come first
not in the standard bibliography
not listed in... but surely a second issue of...
one of an unknown number of copies in this special binding
one of four known states, priority unknown
one of the earliest and perhaps the first
perhaps original, definitely early
possibly a later edition
priority undetermined
probably issued simultaneously with...
the date is suspect and the book probably appeared the following year
the present volume is unrecorded by...

the presumed first printing
there were recurring problems with pirated editions
various dates have been given for this edition
with no date given
wrappers this color not mentioned in the standard bibliography

ENDPAPERS

embroidered silk free endleaves
endpapers reinforced with cloth hinges
endpapers watermarked...
glazed paper endpapers printed in gold
internal endleaves of laid paper
marbled endpapers
original decorated endpapers preserved in rebinding
pictorial endpapers
presentation issue with specially printed endpaper
rice endpapers
silk doublures and endleaves
there is evidence of the front endsheet having been replaced
watered silk endleaves
with endpapers of binder's waste
with scratted paper endpapers

FAULTS - BINDING

a poorly made book
binding a bit skewed
binding scarred but sound
boards gently bowed
disbound with remnants of later backstrip
one signature starting
partly sprung on rear cover
recent unattractive rebinding
several leaves shaved
shelf slanted
some moron used tape to secure the front cover

staining from glue used in binding
stitching broken
the firm stiff back makes opening difficult

FAULTS - COVER DISCOLORED

almost imperceptible fading at edges of boards
covers somewhat smoked
green cloth fading to light brown
irregular fading to boards
label soiled and faded
rear cover discolored
some discoloration to binding
tape shadows on cover and endpapers

FAULTS - COVER STAINS

cloth a little mottled at edges
cloth water damaged
cover sizing is moderately etched
covers a bit marked and dusty
large, but light, dampstain
offsetting to covers from morocco case
outermost board edge stained
ring stain on cover
some soil, it was used
trivial foxing to pastepaper wrappers

FAULTS - COVER TEARS

abrasion at top of front board
front cover torn and chipped
gouge to front cover
large scratch across front cover
piece torn from upper cover
some scratches and abrasions to covers

FAULTS - COVER WEAR

a bit shelf-worn
a few soft creases to rear wrapper

binding shows some signs of use
bumps to vulnerable corners
cloth bubbled on covers
cloth on cover needs replacing
considerable cover wear
covers a trifle bowed
extremities a little worn and frayed
few slight scratches to front cover
labels partly lifted and curled
moderate rubbing and wear to extremities
one corner broken through, board just showing
one corner tender
one cover frayed but this is still a lovely copy
slight wear along top edge of front cover
some corners a bit bruised
somewhat shelf-worn and shaken
touch of shelfwear to bottom edges only
yapp edges worn

FAULTS - DUST JACKET

darkened dust wrapper with only minor edge wear
dust jacket has been insect-nibbled in a few places
dust jacket supplied from another edition
dust jacket with a couple of unobtrusive clean tears
dust wrap is worn along edges but has protected the book well
fragile dust jacket showing only a couple of tiny nicks
glassine wrapper is tanned
in faintly nicked dust jacket
in lightly darkened dust jacket
in spine faded dust jacket
jacket has several creased edge tears
price sliced from dust jacket with small clean cut
small snag in spine of jacket
small sticker peel to jacket
somewhat tired dust jacket
stain visible mostly on unprinted verso of jacket

FAULTS - ENDPAPERS

a couple of tiny staple holes in front free endpaper
discolored endpapers from acid content of binder's glue
endpaper margins stained from binder's glue
endpapers, preliminary and terminal text foxed
endpapers darkened by matter once laid in
endpapers discolored from laid-in newspaper clipping
endpapers slightly mis-glued by binder
faint price sticker trace on endpaper
few imperfections on front pastedowns
free endpapers with natural offsetting
front free endpaper cracking
front pastedown endpaper extends just slightly beyond fore-edge of upper cover
pastedowns and endpapers a little browned from acidic wraps
pastedowns lifting at both fore-edges
small smudge on endpaper
with library card pocket residue on endpaper
with slight lifting of the endpapers

FAULTS - GILT

gilt lettering on spine misprinted
gilt lettering on the spine is notoriously prone to flaking
gilt mostly rubbed from label
gilt partially flaked
some of the gilt has lifted from the tooling
spine gilt oxidized

FAULTS - HINGES

a couple of tiny holes in rear hinge
cloth separating at bottom of hinges
firm but dry
front hinge tender
hairline crack in front hinge
hinges cracked or starting
hinges partially split
front hinge a bit strained

quite mottled along the hinge
shows some cracking but is firm
snag along hinge of front cover
stitchmarks at inner margins
worn and split along one seam

FAULTS - ILLUSTRATIONS

a few chromolithographs with minor surface damage from adhesion
a few plates adhering to each other
a few plates slightly creased in margins
a few plates trimmed to plate-mark
double-page color illustration scraped at gutter
fore-edge painting shows some rubbing
frontispiece and title foxed
light brown spotting on some plates
light offsetting from plates
marginally affecting a few plates
offsetting to most plates
one plate defective
plate facing page 62 has been awkwardly mended
plate strengthened with tape which partially obscures border
plates and guards considerably browned
plates foxed and dampstained
plates oxidized at edges
plates variously foxed
scattered foxing, generally not affecting plates
scattered foxing principally visible on guards
scattered tears causing occasional loss to text or illustrations
several plates have been poorly colored by a previous owner
some illustrations browned
unobtrusive foxing and browning to plates

FAULTS - JOINTS

joints and extremities taped
joints partly chipped and scuffed
lower joint splitting at head
occasional brief wear to joints and ribs

rear joint split but still reasonably sound
small puncture in joint
some wear to joints and edges
trifling split in joint
upper joint somewhat cracked

FAULTS - LOOSE PARTS

a couple of signatures beginning to pull
contents partly loose
covers detached
covers held by one cord only
few gatherings sprung
final gathering loose
front cover becoming loose
frontispiece slightly pulled
generally shaken
loose in binding
one gathering about loose
one map disbound but present
partly loose in binding
rear cover and last few quires detached
several sheets loose because of a fault in binding
signatures a bit strained
some pages loose or frayed
some signature separation
stitching loosening
the stitching has perished
upper cover almost loose
with covers close to coming loose

FAULTS - MINOR

aside from the worn spine, an excellent copy
bright and nearly fine
contents clean except for occasional slight stains
innocuous bump at head of spine
lightest of shelfwear
minor restorations

minor wear to spine
near fine copy of fragile book
normal slight shelf rubbing
not at all bad
occasional slight wear to extremities
only the lightest rubbing at extremities
several small, scarcely detracting holes on spine edges
spine a little worn but the sides in bright and fresh condition
spine ever so lightly sunned
the rubbing of the spine is entirely superficial
very slight surface loss of leather

FAULTS - MISBOUND

bound askew
bound upside-down
first gathering misbound
misbound, with a preliminary gathering bound at the rear
one signature bound backwards
pages set low in the binding
two signatures were reversed when bound

FAULTS - MISSING ILLUSTRATIONS

extra stub-hinges indicate a few plates have probably been removed
lacking one leaf, with stub remaining
lacks the portrait frontispiece
possibly lacking one plate
the chart normally included is not found in this copy
without the full complement of plates

FAULTS - MISSING PARTS

a defective copy with two pages missing
a separate pamphlet of explanatory text, issued with this edition, is not present
apparently lacks first leaf
bound together without a title page
front endsheet neatly excised
front free endpaper removed

integral leaf torn away
lacking pictorial label on upper cover
lacks half-title and errata leaf
lacks last leaf
lacks ties
map not present in rear pocket
spine label lacking
wanting blanks at the beginning and end
wanting flyleaves
with front free endpaper excised

FAULTS - PAGE CREASES

a few leaves ruffled
a few page corners turned down
few leaves wrinkled
final page of text creased
first gathering lightly creased in manufacture
pages lightly damp-rippled; otherwise very good

FAULTS - PAGE DAMAGE

a few glosses slightly cropped
apparent erasure to first title
blank corner of first leaf excised
considerably worn and stained, effacing much of the text
early pages with fraying and loss at edges
fore edges of two leaves cropped
fore-margins of three leaves irregularly cut
insect damage to several leaves
leaves slightly nibbled
lower outer corner off several leaves with slight loss
marginal worming injuring letters in the running heads
pages are slightly cockled
paper flaw affecting a few letters of text
paper in one section is wavy at the top edge
several small chips along gutter where formerly stitched
small portion of title-page cut away affecting dedication
some margins chipped from careless opening

some damage to title page caused by sticking to frontispiece
some loss in corners of leaves, not affecting text
some manuscript marginalia cropped
the top portion of the title-page has been cut away, removing the first word in the title
trimmed a bit close at the top
trimmed close, affecting several headlines
with paperclip mark on several pages
with previous owner's initials in perforation on rear free endpaper
with some fraying of early and late leaves

FAULTS - PAGE STAINS

a bit dusty in the early pages
a few pages with fingersoiling to margins
a largely marginal water stain
cheap paper tanned as usual
contents slight thumbed
corner of cover and all pages stained in upper right
early leaves dampstained
few leaves lightly soiled
fore-edge foxed
leaves browned and brittle at edges
little spotted at the beginning
occasional foxing to terminal leaves
occasional strong offsetting
opening leaves badly dampstained
outer corners dampstained throughout
pages bruised in the calenders
preliminaries slightly damp-stained
some offsetting to facing text
some spotting and offsetting, affecting text more than plates
stain along fore-edge of most pages
tiny rust mark on page one
title page and last page a little browned from acidic wraps

FAULTS - PAGE TEARS

chip due to careless opening, but that portion present on following leaf
clean tear across one text leaf
fore-margin ragged affecting a few letters
leaf torn with some loss of text
marginal chipping on first few leaves
one page carelessly opened
tear in outer margin of one leaf
text leaves incorrectly opened
with some leaves toward the end pulled rather roughly, resulting in short clean tears

FAULTS - SETS

a few covers bumped and worn
a made-up set with some volumes stilted to size
apparent or actual imperfections in this set are...
apparently a made-up set, as Vol. II is taller than Vol. I
chip to one label, else fine
condition varies
first spine just a trifle spotted
front cover detached in first volume
last four leaves defective in first volume
minor worming in two volumes
part of a larger series
shows varying wear
sizes not uniform
spines evenly mellowed
spines faded to an even beige
various bindings

FAULTS - SLIPCASE

in slightly used publisher's slipcase
mismatched cloth slipcase
slipcase age darkened at edges
slipcase imperfect
slipcase is cracked along hinges
slipcase scuffed

FAULTS - SPINE

a bit of fraying to spine
bumped along spine
clear tape stain at spine area
ends of spine a trifle darkened
extremities of spines rubbed
head of spine nicked
leather spine is darker than the rest of the volume, else fine
lettering on spine is partially rubbed off
minor vertical crimp in spine
needs rebacking
old tape stain at foot of spine
part of spine chipped away
red lettering flaked on spine
slight slant
slightly darkened with some wear at ends
spine a little flecked
spine age-darkened and a little rubbed but still a very good copy
spine and top edge of rear cover slightly faded
spine brittle
spine cocked
spine creased and worn at bottom
spine heel abraded
spine label eroded
spine label faded but legible
spine lettering dulled
spine slightly askew
spine tips a little ravelled
tear at foot of spine
vertical split in spine, but holding
with a narrow chip at head of spine
with the spine largely perished

FAULTS - WRITING ADDED

contemporary owner's signature
discreet owner's name on endpaper
few contemporary scrawls on title

marginal ink inscriptions erased
name effaced from front flyleaf
neatly marked by previous owner with colored pencil
numerous ink and pencil annotations including prices
occasional ink or pencil annotations
owner's notations in margins
ownership inkstamp
pencil scribbles on prelims
pencilled inscription in unknown hand
pencilled note in an unidentified hand
some lines of text underlined in ink
with occasional underlining
writing on back shows through

FICTION

a bit of rather lurid fiction
a comic novel
a didactic novel
a famous experimental novel
a keystone of fiction of that era
a rare fantasy work
a satirical novel
a simple story
a tale of fantastic adventure
a yellow-back reprint
an apocryphal story
an epistolary novel
black dialect fiction
intended as light literature
its first appearance was as a three-decker
one of a number of novellas by...
quaint tale of...
recounts the story of...
the further adventures of...
the tale gives the flavor of...

the tale is probably apocryphal
through the medium of fiction he provides a realistic account
with brief and lucid descriptions

FICTION - BIOGRAPHICAL

a fictional autobiography
almost purely autobiographical
an entertaining fictional treatment of his life
invented to add drama to his account
it is semi-autobiographical since...

FICTION -HISTORICAL

a scandalous novel, based entirely on fact
a story with some factual foundation
contains an historical appendix to the novel
fictional history of...
more interesting than formal history, more accurate than fiction

FICTION - MYSTERIES

a futuristic mystery
a masterful detective story
a tale of murder and seduction set in Victorian London
an ingenious thriller
bibliomystery
typical blood-and-thunder thriller
with the style of a traditonal whodunit

FICTION - PRAISE

a first rate adventure story
a pleasant rather unconventional tale
an extraordinary story
considered to be elegant literature
one of the high spots of the literature of the area
one of the most endearing novels of that era
really thrilling at times
tells a charming tale
tells a fascinating tale

the lively tale of...
this story is sure to delight both young and old
weaves a wonderful fictional account around...

FIRSTS

apparently the earliest work on...
contains some political anecdotes never before published
first book appearance
first book giving any information
first book relating exclusively to...
first book written in this country on the subject
first edition in this form
first full-scale description
first of a series of magnificent monographs
first to be published
has not been printed elsewhere
in this volume is published for the first time the complete text
preceded only by an appearance in an anthology
recognized as the earliest full account
the first appearance in book form of anything by...
the first book devoted to...
the first book to concern itself exclusively with...
the first comprehensive review of...
the first major study of this fascinating period
the first mention of...
the first methodical statement
the first to explain why
the first written on a difficult subject
this edition is the first example of this type style
this is the first printed account

FRAGILE

a fragile item, with the paper spine intact
a near fine copy of a book prone to more serious wear
a notoriously fragile book

a rather perishable volume
a very delicate booklet
excellent copy of a fragile binding

HAND WRITTEN NOTATIONS

a few corrections are in evidence
augmented with copious notes
contemporary ink marginalia
decorated with marginal drawings
neat, small nonauthorial name
numerous contemporary margin notations
pencilled bibliographic note on verso of the fly leaf
the marginal entries in manuscript are of interest
wide margins with frequent contemporary annotations
with analytical marginal notes
with ink textual corrections
with neat manuscript notes at the end
with pencil bibliographic notes
with penciled mathematic computations on rear free endpaper
with pencilled substantive corrections in an unknown hand
with two lines of extra manuscript errata

HOW TO

a basic text for those with little or no experience
a good introductory manual
a manual comprised of rules to acquaint the inexperienced with a full knowledge
a practical treatise
an informal explanation
clear, comprehensive guide
contains in-depth how-to-do-it information
contains practical suggestions
described in a step by step manner
equips the reader with all the information needed
for a rational explanation of the principles
gives detailed instructions for repairs and maintenance
illustrates the laborious process

makes a number of suggestions
offers a solid grounding in the fundamental skills
offers a step-by-step explanation
offers tips and stategies
outlines proper technique and describes how to come by it
practical manual written as a series of directions & questions
this coherent handbook will brief readers
this simple book outlines methods of...
to be used as a demonstration
trouble shooting manual
will take the beginner to a position of confidence and skill
with rather careful technical advice

HOW TO - PRAISE

a clear, ready-reference guide
a comprehensive and trusted guide
a knowledgeable guide
a pathbreaking guide
a thoroughly enlightened guide
a valuable source for information
abundant practical advise
an excellent manual
an extremely helpful all-around guide
coherent, professional advise about how to...
convincingly explains
deserves a permanent place on every gardener's bookshelf
everything you ever wanted to know about...
fascinating and instructive book
here is expert advice from the likes of...
offers easy-to-read, practical advice
one of the most sought after manuals
provides expert guidance
reveals the subtleties of technique
technique is discussed with extraordinary clarity and precision
tells the inquisitive reader everything he or she needs to know
the best advice available
there are superb instructions

HUMOR

a grand capacity for irony
a rare attempt at humor by this usually scholarly author
a serious statement presented in a humorous fashion
a thoughtful comedy
a whimsical study
alternately boisterous and facetious comedy
combines intellectual rigor with wit
facetiously presented as a dialogue
filled with amusing and intriguing anecdotes
immensely successful and riotously amusing
keen and deliciously witty
knows how to laugh and make his readers laugh
presents his material with unfailing humor
semi-humorous story
spiced with uproarious wit
the imprint is wholly facetious

ILLUSTRATIONS - ARTIST

engraved double-page frontispiece by the author
first book illustrated from drawings by...
illustrations after designs by...
illustrations hand-colored by the artist throughout
one of the best known works illustrated by...
possibly the first book to be illustrated by...
the artist is a most imaginative illustrator
this book contains more illustrations by... than any other
with added plates by...
with three line drawings by the author

ILLUSTRATIONS - COLORED

a few illustrations, including some in color
filled with tinted linoleum cuts
full-page gouache illustrations painted directly in the book
illustrated using bold color and strong design
including mounted plates in color
numerous chromolithographic plates

one of the earliest books on... with colored illustrations
profusely illustrated, including plates in color
reproduced here in color
the plates are mostly in color
utilizing many color illustrations
with a profusion of color facsimile illustrations
with color lithograph plates and other illustrations
with the coloring of the illustrations done by hand stenciling

ILLUSTRATIONS - CONTENT

a photographic documentation
a richly illustrated survey
an illustrated look at the best in...
an illustrated herbal
contains numerous facsimile letters, sketches and photographs
frontispiece is a diagram
has a strong narrative quality
illustrated with sketches of contemporary events
illustrated with full page facsimiles
many of the illustrations show...
numerous caricature plates
plates of facsimile manuscripts
some plates with two or more images
woodcut illustrations, some with contemporary handcoloring

ILLUSTRATIONS - DRAWINGS

a crayon drawing, signed by...
drawings in pencil with white heightening
full-page watercolor illustrations drawn directly in the book
large ink and watercolor drawings
mixed media sketches
on the half-title is an original pen-and-ink drawing
with detailed scale drawings

ILLUSTRATIONS - EXTRA

a colored suite of the plates on Arches
a Grangerized book, with no added illustrations

accompanied by an extra suite of plates in a separate portfolio
accompanied by a suite of plates not in the book
an additional drawing is neatly pasted to inside front cover
an impressive example of the extra-illustrator's art
includes a photograph not present in the trade edition
several specimen leaves bound in
text inlaid throughout with plates of larger format inserted
with a cancelled suite of the illustrations
with plates inlaid in larger paper to match size of volume

ILLUSTRATIONS - FOLDING

augmented with folding maps
folding plates, each with multiple figures
illustrated with plates and maps, some folding
large folding lithographed plate depicting ...
numerous folding architectural plans
well illustrated including two foldout inserts, one in color
with a center double-spread illustration
with folding charts
woodcut foldout sheet

ILLUSTRATIONS - GUARDS

last two plates guarded
tissue-guarded photogravure illustrations
with engraved captions on the tissue guards

ILLUSTRATIONS - MAPS

contains a fine map of the contemporary U.S.
contains the often missing and sought after map
includes the first geological map of...
including a large unbound folding map
including the atlas of plates
though issued without a map, pirated copies occasionally have one
with the facsimile map
with the original folding map

ILLUSTRATIONS - PHOTOGRAPHS

accompanied by loose photographic reproductions
beautifully photographed and described
color photomontage
illustrated with full page gravures
illustrated with stereoscopic views
in heliogravure and color
produced by the process of photo color relief printing
profusely illustrated with superb gravure plates
replete with movie stills
tipped in photo, captioned in an unknown hand
with a profusion of illustrations from photographs
with original mounted albumen photograph

ILLUSTRATIONS - PORTRAITS

engraved portrait on india paper mounted
mounted color portrait
with a portrait in uncut state
with a self-caricature on the front free endpaper
with portrait frontispiece
with vignettes of silhouettes

ILLUSTRATIONS - PRAISE

a magnificent pictorial record
a most beautiful coffee table book
a superb plate book
a well-illustrated look at...
absolutely striking views of the American Southwest
beautifully and handsomely illustrated
brilliantly illustrated
charming, delicately engraved plates
cleverly illustrated
engravings exquisitely hand-colored by talented artists
fine scenes and views add much to the book
hand-colored engravings with subtle pastel shading
illustrated by beautifully executed engravings
illustrated with stunning detail

illustrated with fine scenes and views
illustrated with plates not readily seen elsewhere
intense and powerful illustrations
lovely little plates given over almost entirely to recording...
luxuriously illustrated
one of the masterpieces of the illustrated book
one of the most sumptuously illustrated books
precisely illustrates
quite a nice color plate for an American book of this period
radiantly colored chromolithographs
sepia frontispiece redrawn by...
show remarkable detail
superbly reproduced
the illustrations stand on their own merit
these plates are better than those in the third edition
with amusing illustrations
with attractive pictorial embellishment
with dramatically engraved plates
with elaborate illustrative scenes

ILLUSTRATIONS - QUANTITY

32 pages of text followed by 96 plates
contains hundreds of illustrations
gives a profusely illustrated glimpse at...
many pages in color
numerous appealing illustrations
profusion of full and half page illustrations
resplendent with many fine engravings
with many illustrations showing examples of...
with three delightful color plates

ILLUSTRATIONS - TEXT COORDINATION

a charming marriage of text and illustrations
a clear elucidation of the text
a number of plates support their scientific conclusions
an excellent manual, greatly aided by the illustrations
beautiful line drawings do full justice to the text

decoratively sums up the author's meaning
each entry is complemented by an abstact illustration
her illustrations give bold embodiment to the text
his illustrations are a natural complement to these tales
illustrated with photographs by the author
illustrated with explanatory text
in harmony with the text
keeping step with the illustrator
letterpress relating to each plate is on the verso of the preceding plate
made expressly for this work
meshes neatly with the tale
photographs illustrate every step of every process described
the illustrations express all the humor of the text
well-illustrated discussion of...
with facing leaf of letterpress text
with notes and descriptions on the woodcuts
with run round illustrations on most pages

ILLUSTRATIONS - TITLE PAGE

apart from the title-page it is unillustrated
copperplate title page with vignette
elaborate historiated title in sepia watercolor
engraved divisional titles
engraved title vignettes and dedication
hand illuminated title page decorations
ornamental title page
title page with impressed floral design
title within typographical borders
with a double frontispiece in full color
with an engraved title
with crible' and strapwork title border
with ornate title page design
with pictorial border to title page
woodcut ornament on title

ILLUSTRATIONS - UNCOLORED

illustrated in cut paper silhouettes
illustrated with half tones
illustrations in uncolored state
uncolored schematic plate
uncolored text illustrations, some full page
with uncolored plates

IMPORTANCE

a famous manifesto
a foundation book
a very significant copy of this key volume
an astonishing and important work
an early and important statement
an essential volume for the devotee of...
an important book in its own right
constitutes the cornerstone of...
essentially the definitive text
has become a bible for...
immediately relevant to the present
importance is shown by the constant reprints
important because it is such an early account
indispensable to a full understanding
its place in literary history is secure
one of the major works of the period
one of the truly important books of its day
remains the definitive study
representative of a significant trend in literature
should be in the library of every bibliophile
the neglect of this subject up until now is scandalous
the points made in this pivotal work are still compelling
won the Pulitzer Prize

IMPORTANCE - SUPERLATIVES

one of the most important works ever attempted
the most important such work to come to us from that time
the most significant document relative to...

the most valuable record of...
the significance of this copy is difficult to overestimate
this book will change your life

INFLUENCE

a key book in the development of...
a pioneering book which brings to light...
a valuable contribution to our knowledge
an immensely influential work of theological thought
an influential book of its kind
awakened public interest
brought a dramatic change in the public's awareness
changed the course of history
created a national awareness
demonstrates the growing influence
did the most to influence the direction of...
established the issues of economic thought for generations to come
few books have exercised a more profound influence
greatly raised the standards of...
it laid the groundwork
its publication led to...
laid the foundation for modern thought
modern readers still derive inspiration from...
often cited
one of the most influential prose works of the 19th century
reflects the converging influences of...
served as a considerable stimulus
sparked great interest in this vital subject
this pioneering work led to a greater appreciation
this work played an essential role
widely reprinted, its views proved influential

INSCRIPTIONS

a difficult book to locate inscribed
additionally inscribed at the colophon
bears a wonderful long inscription
brief inscription in gutter of title page

inked presentation inscription
inscribed, with a portion of the inscription excised
inscribed by the author with a sketch
inscribed on a card affixed to front free endpaper
inscribed on front free endpaper in the month of publication
inscribed to an academic mentor
inscribed with a quotation from the book
inscription is probably near contemporary with publication
inscription is dated within a month of publication
inscriptions of this vintage are few and far between
lengthy inscription on flyleaf
nearly illegible contemporary ink inscription
the recipient is unidentified in the inscription, but may be...
with a curious inscription on the half-title
with a warm full-page presentation inscription
with a wonderful inscription on the half-title
with an apparently contemporary inscription
with an intimate inscription

INSERTIONS - AUTOGRAPHS

autograph signature clipped from a larger document and mounted
clipped signature neatly affixed at the bottom of the page
signed document tipped in
with typed letter, signed, taped to rear endpaper

INSERTIONS - CLIPPINGS

many relevant clippings and notes loosely inserted
numerous clippings neatly attached to the blanks
obituary of author tipped in at rear
periodical clippings about the author laid in
related contemporary newspaper cutting tipped in
with a brief review glued to the front inside panel of dustwrap

INSERTIONS - MOUNTED

bookseller sticker on front endpaper
mounted to size (possibly inserted from a smaller copy)
presentation plate mounted to front pastedown

tipped to a stub at the back of the book
with a mounted pencil drawing
with the original bookseller's label replaced on pastedown

INSERTIONS - PUBLISHER'S

a separate leaf of volvelles at the end
a signed and numbered copy of the portrait is laid in, as called for in the colophon
attached is a tabula in four leaves
certificate of issue pasted to inside front cover
corrected map mounted inside rear wrapper
errata slip present but no corrections made to the text
promotional material stapled in front
publisher's ticket on rear pastedown
specimen mounted on title page
specimen pages included
with an inserted preliminary
with sewn-in ribbon markers
with the rare printed announcement slip
with the sheet of binder's instructions laid in

INSERTIONS - OTHER

letter laid in which gives an estimate of the book's value
receipt for the book laid in
small bookseller's description partly mounted on title
with an unrelated letter
with some appropriate ephemera laid in

INSTITUTIONAL MARKS

card pocket affixed to paste down
discreet embossed library stamp
ex-library
French export stamp in bottom margin
inked library stamps on title and final leaf
institutional bookplate (deaccessioned)
institutional rubberstamp on verso eradicated
library number effaced from spine

neat library withdrawal stamp but no other ex-libris markings
scattered library stamps erased
shelfmark on front pastedown
tiny deaccession stamp on verso of title
with call number on spine

INTENT

a celebratory book, intended to please rather than to persuade
a classical interpretation of the philosophy
a discussion of the problems he encountered
a not too serious look into...
a theoretical and practical treatise
an attempt to depict the nature of...
an examination of the psyche
an inquiry into the truth of certain allegations
bridges the gaps of prior writings on the subject
designed to give an in-depth understanding
explanation and defense of...
from the title, it appears to have been intended for...
he speculates herein on the reasons
heavily provided with morals
his intention was to illuminate the part he played
his stated object in writing this work was...
intended for the coffee table
intended to condemn, it misfires and is very amusing
intended to improve our minds and morals
intended to please rather than persuade
issued to demonstrate that...
its main purpose was to instruct
largely a vehicle for the expression of...
meant to clarify
produced as a tribute
published to meet the demand
speaks to the business needs
the author's intention was to provide...
the author's stated purpose is...
the chief intent of this book lies in...

the paramount issue reflected in the work is...
to demonstrate advances in...
to explore the need for an analysis of the subject in depth
to fill the gaps in our knowledge
to gain cultural and historical perspective
to give a lucid discussion
to give a vivid picture of conditions
to give contemporary discussions
to narrow the definition
to provide an apology
to provide insight into aspects of...
to provide the most striking evidence
to satisfy a particular challenge
to satisfy the obvious need
to speculate on the possibilities
written as an antithesis
written to impart a deeper understanding

INTERESTING

a book to savor
a compelling account
a fascinating book textually
a marvelous read
a most enjoyable way to study the work of...
a most satisfying read
a possibly fictional and certainly entertaining account of...
a rousing account
additional interest attaches to this narrative because of...
an absorbing tale
an action-packed account
an entertaining and enlightening view
an evocative story
an exceptionally enjoyable volume
an unforgettable testament
as entertaining as it is informative
cheerful reading
compelling reading

here is a book which will fascinate the reader
in depth and eminently readable
intensely interesting to readers
interesting observations on...
juicy tidbits
makes the subject enthralling to the layman
must reading
one can imagine the readers poring over this
superb reading
tells the fascinating story in an entertaining manner
the information is presented in a very readable format
this is perfect for vacation reading
will awe even the most demanding reader
worth reading for sheer entertainment
worth reading and rereading

INTRODUCTION

a tantalizing introduction
edited with a note by...
prefatory verse
sets the stage
the introduction fills two pages of a bifolium sheet
the recommendatory address is by...
the substantial introduction discusses...
with a new introduction for this limited edition
with a preface written by the author expressly for this edition
with a presentation from the author
with ample commentary by...
with an appreciative introductory essay
with an ingenious introduction
with an inspiring introduction
with an introduction and a final note

MANUSCRIPTS

a clean typescript with no corrections
a first draft manuscript with frequent substantive insertions, deletions and corrections

a manuscript in his handwriting
a tantalizing manuscript
holograph manuscript with pencil revisions in another hand
manuscript shows numerous deletions and corrections throughout
the author's own set of page proofs
the original working file for...
very rough draft
with a carbon typescript of the final draft
with a few minor manuscript corrections
with numerous authorial changes throughout the text
with the author's emendations as sent to the printer

MASTERPIECE

a classic in its field
a landmark book
a literary masterpiece
a masterpiece of its kind
a minor classic of the time
a pivotal work in the author's canon
a towering classic
among the greatest novels since the inception of the form
an enduring classic
believed by many to be a masterpiece
considered to be the most well written novels of the period
generally regarded as his masterpiece
has been described as ...'s greatest work
his major achievement
it is indeed a magnum opus
it is the great work on which his fame rests
one of a handful of novels of the era likely to stand the test of time
perhaps his grandest achievement
recognized as a seminal work
the basis of his reputation
widely considered her best work

NONFICTION

a factual account
a rarely found pioneer narrative
a recounting of one of the most infamous trials of the century
a scarce early nonfiction work
almanac style
an album of factual murder cases, still unsolved
an authoritative odyssey through the fascinating world of...
an introduction to the study of...
authentic and thrilling narrative
based on a searching inquiry
has the unerring ring of truth
intriguing stories delved from obscure sources
possesses the drama of a novel
relates an anecdote
rich in facts relating to...
shows the origin
the first trustworthy account

OUT OF PRINT

completely sold out upon publication
has been out of print for a number of years
in print technically, but out of stock for some months now
it was almost out of print on publication
long out of print and scarce
no longer available from the publisher
now out of print but still at in-print price
oversubscribed at publication and now difficult to locate
published in a small edition and already somewhat scarce
rare due to an inadequate print-run
rare item due to the low limitation and private distribution
reprinted from 1900 to 1920
the original printing is a very difficult book to obtain
the small first printing was quickly exhausted
very limited issue, entirely sold out

PAGE DECORATION

a background over which the type is printed
adorned with morisques
decorative head and tail pieces
different decorative borders on every page
divisional woodcut titles
liberal use of decorative headpieces
linocut text ornaments and vignettes
metalcut borders on every page
ornamental headpieces and pictorial tailpieces
pictorial device on the limitation statement
the pages are boxed-in
with a canting mark on the colophon
with a recurring decoration
with cock-up initials
with color ornamentation
with cut-in heads
with entrelac initials
with fac initials
with many engaging drolleries in the outer margins
woodcut historiated border

PAGE REPAIRS

clean tear in leaf, patched
endpapers renewed
first two leaves remargined at gutter
fore-edge corners repaired
numerous leaves washed
outer leaves taped in gutter
outer margin of first twelve leaves expertly repaired
skillfully extended to size (provided from another copy)
some reinforcement to chipped pages
some text and border supplied in ink
the three pages which were re-set are slightly out of alignment
title partially backed with new paper
title-leaf rehinged
trimmed letters are completed in pen facsimile

with a few torn margins patched
with several pages silked
with the title-page and frontispiece extended at the inner margins

PAGINATION

inserted facsimile included in pagination
margins trimmed, with loss of pagination
non-sequential pagination
not paginated but over 100 pages
paginated irregularly
second gathering incorrectly imposed, resulting in erratic (but complete)
pagination
the pagination is continuous
unfoliated and unsigned
with an occasional hiatus in numbering
with six unpaginated leaves between pages 14 and 15

POETIC

a portion of the narrative is in the form of a poem
colorful facts set forth in verse
conjures visions of...
described in the purest poetry
flawless prose
highly lyrical
in Italian macaronic verse
the text is in rhymed couplets

POINT OF VIEW

a first-hand chronicle
a highly subjective portrait
a journalistic account
an expert talking shop
an eyewitness account of events of great magnitude
an impartial account
characteristic mixture of realistic and fantasy elements
devoted to presenting his position

from his vantagepoint
from the point of view of...
keenly impersonal narrative
obliquely approached
one of the best first-hand studies
remarkably detailed first-hand account
text of this work is an interior monologue
the narrative point of view alternates between...
the reader is led into that special world through his eyes
the subject is allowed to speak for himself
this unique, personal account
through his experienced eyes, we see...
written in the first person

POINTS

a bibliographically interesting copy
mixed first and second printing, with 6 of 13 points
of several variant issues, this is as described by...
tabulation of variant editions comparing points of difference
the press corrections would indicate a second state
title page is a variant not cited in...
variant wraps or a bibliographer's error
with 2 first state points
with battered page numeral on page...
with points of first issue
with the bastard "g" on page 82
with the broken descender on the "g"
with the clogged "a" on page...
without the imprimatur on the verso of the title page

POINTS - BINDING

first issue binding
first state of both text and binding
probable first binding state
very scarce variant binding
with yellow and green headbands

POINTS - MISTAKES

corrected in subsequent printings
one running-title printed upside-down
the usual second issue with the misprint corrected
this mistake occurred only in the earliest copies
was inadvertently omitted from the earliest copies only
with the fourth line doubled

POPULARITY

a highly popular overview
a non-academic text makes this book accessible
a popular and informative work
a popular book several times reprinted
a sought-after book
a surprise bestseller
a well-received novel
achieved sensational impact
almost immediately out of print
greatly admired by such later writers as...
had a great success on the stage
it has always been amazingly popular
soon became a collectible edition
the basis for the popular film
the book was an immediate success
the first of his books to achieve favorable public notice
the text proved popular and went quickly through three editions
undoubtedly the most often read
was widely read

PRAISE

a highly esteemed book
a readable, well illustrated pamphlet
a remarkable statement
a remarkable testament
a rollicking good book
a thought provoking, philosophical work
a trenchant treatise

a wonderful compendium
after all these years, this book still stands on its own merits
an impressive and worthwhile book
an unparalleled account
beautifully chronicled
best book on the subject
graceful book of great beauty
has the air of a classic
highly praised
it certainly is a fitting tribute
offers remarkable insight
outstanding copy of a fascinating book
the most useful book ever published
the verisimilitude is startling
this book will be cherished
this book's a dandy
you don't encounter many books this good

PREPUBLICATION COPY

a dirty proof of his first book
a marked proof
a number of emendations were made in the final published version
collating this proof with the finished book shows many significant differences
complete proof impression
differs considerably and significantly from the final version
differs in many respects from its final published version
not collated for possible variations between this and the published text
pre-publication galleys bound in pad form as issued
pre-publicity proof from uncorrected galleys
printer's annotated copy
proof sheets with numerous directions to the printer
publisher's dummy of the first edition
spiral bound proof which is usually prepared in small numbers
typed interim version

uncorrected trimmed long galleys of the first edition
with a variant title from the final form
with indications of type style and size and galley number

PROPAGANDA

a piece of bare-faced propaganda
an appeal on behalf of...
argues in favor of...
blatantly laden with moral baggage
coming down heavily in favor of...
consciously moralistic
defensive self-justification
espousing the unlikely concept of...
extolls the virtues of...
issued as a promotional pamphlet
it particularly argues for...

PROVENANCE

a note records the presentation of the volume to...
bought from Rosenbach
by direct descent to...
during which time the books have been in the possession of...
from the personal collection of the noted bibliophile...
has a rather notable provenance
has always been in the possession of...
has the ownership inscription of...
illustrated ownership inscription on endpaper
inscribed to...with the recipient's bookplate
name embossed on title page
owner's insignia on title page
owner's mark branded on upper and bottom edges
passed to her only child
pencilled note states it was bought at the ... sale
previous owner's ink inscription on flyleaf
...'s copy, according to pencilled note
said to be from the library of...
the books were inherited by...

the recipient was an important client
the recipient was himself a writer of fiction
title with old ownership stamp
was formerly in the possession of...
with a provenance tracing this copy back to the original owner
with an unsigned presentation inscription
with his perforated stamp on title
with the bookplate of the recipient

PROVENANCE UNCERTAIN

anonymous owner
the provenance is probable but unconfirmed
the recipient of this book is probably a member of the family
the recipient might have been...
unfortunately there is no evidence of provenance
unidentified sixteenth-century monastic inscription

PUBLISHER

compiled by... and published by...
known as printer to the scientific world
of note chiefly due to the imprint
printer's woodcut device on title
publisher's stamp in blind on back cover
with many imprints to his credit

PUBLISHER - EARLY

first large scale production completely produced at the press
first put to press by...
known for issuing many firsts in printing history
one of the first printings from...
one of the only books published by...
the first U.S. publisher to specialize in...
very early example of Chiswick Press color printing
was once this country's most influential publishing house

PUBLISHER - PRAISE

a most skillful practitioner of the handpress
an outstanding achievement of nineteenth century printing
beautifully printed and bound at the Grabhorn Press
demonstrated fastidious care in its production
has produced work of superb quality if in no great volume
one of the great works of this press
one of the highpoints of the press
one of the loveliest volumes produced by...
one of the masterpieces of the press
one of the more spectacularly produced books from this press
produced with amazing virtuosity
the chef d'oeuvre of this press
took care in the typographic appearance of his productions
took great pride in producing books of this quality
well-printed by...

PUBLISHER - PRIVATE

not printed for sale
printed entirely at the author's expense
printed rather amateurishly
probably printed at his own expense
produced under the auspices of...
published by the authors
virtually privately published

PUBLISHER - RARE

a highly unusual imprint
imprints from this press are extremely rare
unrecorded in the checklist for this imprint

RARE

a bibliographical rarity with a fabulous association
a modestly uncommon book
a scarce early nonfiction work by this mostly fiction author
a very good copy of a scarce book
an appealing and uncommon book

an elusive title
even the regular issue of this title is scarce
fresh, sound copy of this rare edition
legendary rarity of modern literature
never a particularly easy book to come by
no other copy has been offered at auction since...
not normally found separately
not recorded in any of the usual bibliographies
of 500 copies, 200 unsold copies were later destroyed
one of his more elusive works
one of the author's most difficult books to locate
one of the noted rarities of modern literature
reportedly only 500 copies were distributed
scarce in any printing
scarce in any edition
seldom appears on the market
surprisingly scarce title
the author's rare first published work
the first printing was quickly oversubscribed
the most desireable and most elusive limited edition
the only copy we have offered with the scarce inscription
the publisher opted for a small first printing
this book had a limited distribution in this country

RAREST

a fine copy of author's rarest work
a recent census has accounted for only six copies
all editions are very scarce
all known copies seem to be in public collections
appears to be one of the rarest books published by...
appears to be the only complete early edition sold recently
books don't get much scarcer than this
catalogue description laid in, describing this as the only known copy
few copies survive today and no two are alike
one of the holy grails of book collecting

one of the rarest of the special editions produced by this press
one of the scarcest items in the author's canon
only six copies of this book were sold before it was withdrawn

READING COPY

a good second-hand copy only
a working copy at best
has been read to pieces
sound and complete

REFERENCE

a directory of...
a primary source for others to follow
a standard reference work
a supportive reference collection
a unique primary source
a useful collection description-cum-bibliography
a useful compendium
a valuable, if somewhat general, reference work
all the answers to all your questions
an encyclopedic guide
an enormous amount of information can be found here
an essential reference tool
an important source book for those interested in...
bibliophile reference work
contains all the topics that normally constitute...
contains many interesting facts concerning...
contains vast amounts of information
copiously annotated
for many years this was the standard work on the subject
frequently cited
has often been consulted by scholars
much of this information is not readily accessible elsewhere
the basic standard reference on the subject
the most all-encompassing compendium of information
the source from which most accounts have been drawn
the usefulness of this volume is enhanced by indices and appendices

REFERENCE - HISTORICAL

a chronicle of one of the most famous sea battles of the war
a chronological compendium of historical documents
a chronological checklist
a comprehensive study which traces the growth
a constant source for later historians
a contemporary history
a fascinating look at this historical period
a look at developments
a pictorial history
a regional history
a thorough study of the beginning and development
a virtual storehouse of historical information
a visual history
an historical and technical essay
an important cache of historical information
contains details of the localities, events, and personalities of the war
covers the development and history
demonstrates a profound sense of history
examines the technological history
for an understanding of the historical role
historically important for its view
invaluable to the social historian
it disseminates information on the history and lore
one of the great narratives of exploration
organized both chronologically and geographically
provides commentary and historical background
reveals much about early American life and thought
traces the evolution
with notes historical, critical and biographical
100 pages of pure historical pleasure

REFERENCE - PRAISE

a lucid and worthwhile history of the city
a particularly valuable source
a pithy reference manual
a treasure house of historic detail

a wonderfully informative reference source
an excellent contemporary source of information
an excellent reference guide with commentary
an important tool in the study of...
an impressive guide to the history of...
densely packed with practical information
essential reference work
first historically precise description
indispensible to the student
one of the great and ageless historical works
revealing and historically significant
still one of the best of the bibliographies of this author
the best bibliographic tool available
the most accurate account of the period

REMAINDERS

a remaindered edition
faint remainder mark on bottom edge

REVIEW COPY

a press proof
a review copy, so marked in perforation
advance reading copy from uncorrected proofs
advance review copy with the publisher's slip laid in
advance state of the first edition, for review
complimentary advance copy, so stated on special endpapers
early presentation copy, preceding the official publication date
in advance issue dust jacket
special prepublication issue for American booksellers

SATIRE

a bit of social satire
a biting look at...
a bitter satire on the author's own age
a colloection of satirical parodies
a parody
a playful satire

a political satire
a satirical harlequinade
a tongue in cheek comment
a vehicle for propaganda
actually a spoof
his characters are thinly disguised political figures of the time
makes sport of...
nobody emerges unscathed
satirical and facetious

SCHOLARLY

was conceived as a satirical attack
a classic, scholarly work
a comprehensive view of the field up to that point
a definitive work
a major study summarizing his work
a massive scholarly survey
a reliable investigation
a scholarly work which explains a great deal
a serious examination
a storehouse of information concerning...
a study concerned with the psychological aspects
an authoritative compilation
an influential polemic
any academic library ought to own one
came by the information authoritatively
drew upon this book extensively
filled with a vast amount of valuable material
for a full description of the complexities
has lengthy text citations
includes much information not appearing elsewhere
it is a rigorous examination
lengthy and well researched
many technical articles
massively supported by documents, charts and maps
one of the first cases of scholarship applied to...
ought to stimulate further research and writing

presents the core material
provides all the background material necessary
richly annotated
sound scientific data
the only full-length completely documented study
the text is supported by indexes and appendices
the text presents the fruits of his research
thoroughly annotated and indexed
with notes containing a vast amount of information

SCHOLARLY - PRAISE

a monument of erudition
a rich resource for scholarship and learning
a scrupulous examination
a thoughtful work displaying diligent research
a valuable and broad treatise
a vastly informative book
an esteemed study of the subject
an excellent, scholarly study
an incisive study
an inspired journalistic study
brilliantly answers complex questions
comprehensive and learned
displays his great erudition
entertaining yet scholarly
has been heralded as a landmark study
indispensible to any study of the subject
not only a very good book, but also a substantial one on the topic
notable for its scholarship
of value as a resource
one of the greatest of all medical classics
scholarly and fascinating
splendidly researched
the best anatomical textbook available at the time
the definitive work to-date
the latest state of the art technology

the most exhaustive and the best
vivid description interwoven with scientific observation
widely considered to be the classic in the field

SERIAL PUBLICATION

a broken run of this periodical
a college humor magazine
a complete run of this iconoclastic magazine
a long run of an uncommon series
a merititious literary magazine
a representative gathering of issues
a slightly broken run, consisting of...
an important venue for the introduction of new writing
anniversary issue
another good book from an excellent series
complete runs of this publication have become somewhat scarce
each part issued separately and subsequently bound up
in the original parts
issued monthly in six parts
meant to be a companion volume
published monthly in groups of ten
several issues of this short-lived periodical
the extremely uncommon initial issue
the first of the series
the promised sequels never reached fruition
written as a supplement to his earlier work

SETS - COMPLETE

a complete file of the original series
a complete run
a third volume, although called for, was never published
in stilted covers to conform with the set
issued as a three-decker
the only known complete set
thirteen volumes in twelve
together, two volumes

two parts in one volume
two volumes bound as one
uninterrupted set

SETS - INCOMPLETE

a set of 6 volumes (only)
complete sets are rare because it was issued over several years
sets like this have nearly all been broken
the first volume only of four
the present set consists of the following...
the second book in a planned trilogy
this set is very difficult to find complete in fine bindings

SETS - PRAISE

a fabulous set
a fine fresh set, entirely uncut
a good sound set
a handsome set delightfully illustrated throughout
a lovely set in original condition
a magnificent collection of books
a sparkling set
an outstanding children's set
certainly a very good set
excellent group of twelve volumes
mint set in custom boxes
remarkably fine set
sound set of this monumental series

SIZE - FOLIO

a folio with thick creamy paper
a landscape folio
an imposing folio
elephant folio atlas
imperial folio
small narrow folio

SIZE - LARGE

a fine, clean, tall copy
a large, elegant volume
a massive book covering all aspects
a tome
an elongated book
an excellent copy of this massive novel
an extremely important and voluminous archive
hefty, sizeable volume
large thick 4to
large-paper copy
monumental and compelling
oversized paperback
too large to read in bed
with pages bulking 1 3/4"

SIZE - SMALL

a miniature edition
a narrow copy
a set of 20 volumes, 12mo et infra
an early duodecimo printing
an exquisite bibelot
a slim little booklet
compact and easy to carry
excellent little book
in miniature format
pocket edition
rests comfortably in your hand
the entire novel occupies only 96 pages
thin 48mo
thin paper copy
very thick 12mo

SLIPCASE

enclosed in a morocco-backed protective clamshell box
half buckram folder
high quality protective cover

housed in a handsome clamshell box-case
in a custom calf folder
in a rather primitive cardboard clamshell box
in an elaborate folding slipcase
in an elaborately jewelled cumdach
in an ornamental coffin
in bruised publisher's slipcase
in double compartment slipcase
in fleece-lined cloth box
in newly made slipcase closely matching the original
in original fitted case
in publisher's pictorial box
in vellum-backed tray case
loose in half leather portfolio
loose in uniformly bound slipcase
marbled board folding hand-lettered case
mint copy in repaired box
pigskin solander cases
red plush lined folding case with inset for pamphlet
three volumes in one slipcase
unbound signatures laid in a full leather case
with a marbled paper box designed to house the entire set

SUPERLATIVES

best book on the subject
by far the most ambitious of his books
deservedly reckoned one of the most brilliant
his celebrated and best known work
his first and most successful work
his most significant work
one of the best books of its kind
one of the great literary works of its time
one of the most innovative and unique specimens ever produced
simply the best there is on the subject
the most accurate account of the period
undoubtedly one of his best works of fiction

TARGET AUDIENCE - CHILDREN

designed to educate and indoctrinate the youngsters
done in the format of a primer for children
he had children especially in mind
heavily edited for a juvenile audience
intended as instruction for children
originally for the use of children

TARGET AUDIENCE - EDUCATIONAL

addressed to the serious laymen
a feast for all serious bibliophiles everywhere
an essential addition to your library
for the beginner as well as the experienced
for the student of history
for those seeking a better understanding
indispensible to the student
intelligible to both the layman and specialist
is extremely useful to students

TARGET AUDIENCE - OTHER

an indispensible book for those interested in...
for Texas enthusiasts
he addresses himself to...
is devoted solely to...
meant for a mature audience
of much interest to anyone concerned with...
printed for distribution to members
published with the advertiser in mind
special issues intended primarily for... were prepared
this book belongs on every writer's desk
will be a boon to...
will serve an acute need among professionals in the field
written to appeal to...

THOROUGH

a compendious attempt
a comprehensive survey

a copious delineation
a lavish treatise
a mine of information
a minute and correct account
a much more detailed account than has appeared to date
a thorough, documented, and highly detailed examination
an extensive listing
an in-depth examination
covering every aspect
described here in considerable detail
everything you need to know
has encyclopaedic range
most complete and exhaustive work of its kind
most thorough work on the subject
recognized as the most thorough
replete with his encompassing knowledge of the subject
speaks in detail
surprisingly complete and accurate
the most extensive account of its period

TIME PERIOD

a remarkable account of the events immediately following...
a very early appraisal
although written in 18.., it remains fresh and true today
an early Civil War short story
an important contribution to 18th century literature
an interesting history written before...
an invaluable record of the writer's times
contemporary chronology of the important events of...
covering the period from... to...
definitive work at the time
fairly early discussion of...
greatest book on... for the period
his last work was published unfinished, posthumously
literature of the period was typified by...
one of the best contemporary accounts of...
preserves the state of thought on the subject at the time

provides a view into the world of the early 18th century
provides great insight into the temper of the times
published at about the same time as...
summary of contemporary methods
typical of publications of the period, but of interest
viewed through the perspective of fifty years
written while communism was in full flower

TRANSLATIONS

a brilliant translation of this substantial work
a classic translation
a new translation based on recently discovered texts
a powerful new translation
an accurate and lyrical translation
an elegant and faithful translation
first complete edition in English
foreign and late editions were produced
in this translation he has sought to make the difficult text more accessible
rather freely translated
rendered into modern English
reprinted from the French edition
said to be the first translation
text in English and French
the first polyglot edition
the translation into English is unattributed
the translation is a classic in its own right
traditional Hebrew as well as modern texts
translated anonymously
translated from the original, now lost
translated into many languages
was widely translated
with grammatical analysis, commentary and Latin paraphrase
with interlinear translation
with texts in Italian and English on facing pages

TRAVEL GUIDES

a chatty and observant guide to the people and places
a crisp, practical guide
a legendary travel guide
a portrait of a stubborn corner of the American mosaic
a thoughtfully selected list of places to visit
a warm, deep look at a region that has maintained its startling idiosyncracies
a witty and tender look at the country and its citizens
an evocative guide to the region
an informative and entertaining guide
captures the essence of the ancient city
contains much sensible advise to the traveller
gives a vivid overview of the history and culture of the area
no better guide can be found
one of the great narratives of transcontinental travel
picturesque and literate travel guide
simplifies the most puzzling aspects of foreign travel
skillfully reveals a sense of place
takes the reader into the natural habitat of...
targeted for the independent tourist
very basic guidebook
vivid word-pictures make the places come alive
worldwide travel-related excerpts

TYPOGRAPHER

arranged in type by...
ascribed to the ... press on the evidence of the type
created books of beauty
set in type designed by Bruce Rogers
hand-set in foundry Bulmer type

TYPOGRAPHY

headline printed in a large ornamental display type
in half-sheet imposition
newly set into type for the members of the LEC
printed from rubber stamps

printed from type cast from the original matrices
printed from typographic plans
printed in Centaur by hand
printed in period style
printed in roman and italic types
printed in two colors throughout
reflects the bold typography typical of this printer
set in Caslon Old-Face type
set in movable type
text in parallel columns of Greek and Latin
text in two columns in roman
text is set out in oldstyle majuscules
the origin of this edition is suggested by the typography
the typographical appearance is consistent with that period
title within typographical borders
with closely printed pages
woodcut initials and decorations after the style of...

TYPOGRAPHY - CALLIGRAPHY

calligraphic title
hand-lettered text
the text is calligraphic
typeface is designed to mimic handwriting
wholly in the calligraphy of...

TYPOGRAPHY - CRITICISM

badly put together typographically
in a very cramped and hard-to-read type-face
not up to his usual standards of typography
over-weighted and over embellished
the ink has feathered on the open-grained paper
the typeface is especially distracting
there is some show through

TYPOGRAPHY - INNOVATION

avant-garde typography
experimental typographical layouts complement the text

set in assorted exotic types
the latest word in type fashion
the type was especially cast for this work
this is only the second use of this typeface
unusual colophon
very attractive and uncommon in format and design

TYPOGRAPHY - PRAISE

a very important book in a handsome format
a wonderful display of typographic skill
achieves a clean letterpress impression
an example of printing by one of the better known houses
an excellent display of American typography
beautifully displays sophisticated typography
best type quality throughout
carefully chosen type
filled with interesting typographic arrangements
handsomely printed in Caslon type
highly imaginative design work
imaginative design gives this book a timeless quality
impeccably produced
lavishly illustrated with type specimens
nicely printed early work on the subject
one of the books he admired most of all his designs
one of the most typographically pleasing books of the period
praised for the quality of its printing
shows sensitivity to letter spacing
shows unusual concern for typography and design
the pride of the printer comes through
typographically pleasing
with careful layout and letter spacing
with delicately composed text
with well spaced Caslon capitals

UNOPENED

in new unopened condition
partly unopened
uncut and largely unopened
with a couple of head bolts uncut

WRITING - COMPARISON

here he writes with more confidence than before
one is reminded of..., but... is certainly his own author
written in a style reminiscent of...
written in the tradition of great rural essayists

WRITING - PRAISE

a brilliant and effective piece of writing
a fascinating and enlightening commentary
a masterpiece of description
a powerful piece of political and social commentary
a sharp and appreciative view
an insightful commentary which skillfully traces...
brimming with infectious humanity
carefully written
contains splendid writing
crystal clear and well reasoned
described clearly and concisely
expresses his creative genius
gripping and exhilarating in its analytical detail
in one particularly enticing passage...
light hearted and colorful
lucid, logical presentation
possesses considerable literary merit
provides a realistic immediacy
rich in character and anecdote
the very best writing
the vitality of his writing is quite remarkable
written with a strong plan and construction of the story
written with consistency and style

WRITING STYLE

a fluid and engaging style
a lively anecdotal account
a mixture of the intellectual and the sentimental
an absence of sentimental rhetoric
an impressionistic account
arcane and witty narrative
considered elegant literature
friendly and conversational in tone
goes on at length
he approaches his subject with the utmost seriousness
highly finished style
in a conversational bantering style
in easy to absorb fashion
lively, fresh and unconventional
provocative and entertaining
racy in style
steeped in local atmosphere
the no-holds-barred story
this folksy narrative
told with a distinguishing candor
told with breadth and erudition
told with restraint
written in a sardonic manner
written in a temperate vein

WRITING STYLE - EMOTIONAL

a breathless account
a dark and tragic tale
a funny and sometimes wrenching account
a haunting, heartfelt memoir
a most sympathetic appraisal
a sentimental tale of passion
allowed himself a moment of sentimentality
an impassioned plea
infectious enthusiasm for his subject
melancholy narrative

speaks straight to the heart
there is a certain note of bitterness
told with childlike delight
with a lamentable absence of emotion
with a unique sense of wonder
written from the heart
written in an effusive style
written with compassion and enthusiasm

Author

ACHIEVEMENTS

a book which neatly capped the career of...
a modern master
achieved eminence in his field
achieved some of the most impressive results
both author and designer of books
distinguished for his intelligence
distinguished himself during...
earned respect and affection
established as a leading writer of...
had the field to himself
he virtually invented a new style of fiction
his enduring contribution was...
his greatest life accomplishment was...
his one indubitable accomplishment was...
his supreme achievement is...
rose to literary and social prominence
self-taught
the primary founder of...
the youngest author to be awarded...

ADVOCACY

a dominant early force
a leading proponent of...
a very active force in...
advanced the cause of...
always an advocate of...
an accomplished and successful transformer
an enthusiast of numerous disciplines
champion of the oppressed
driven by his passion for...

encouraged the lavish use of...
gives an indication of the author's later attitude toward...
he became enchanted with...
he boldly advocated extreme measures
his work provided a special stimulus to...
one of the early enthusiasts for...
she devoted her life to proving that...
the guiding spirit behind...

ANONYMOUS

almost surely by...
ascription of authorship does not appear in any of the usual places
authorship was not known until early this century
authorship was questioned for years
credited to... but this seems to be an error
frequently been attributed to...
ghost-authored
his actual connection with this work is doubtful
later scholars suggest... as the author
likely to have been written by...
may be by the same hand as...
modern research has finally exposed... as the author
more than likely prepared by...
most often attributed to...
no name given
no one has made claim to the authorship
of doubtful authorship
often falsely attributed to...
persistently ascribed, on stylistic grounds to...
possibly written by...but also attributed to...
probably ghost-written by...
purported to have been written, at least in part, by...
the evidence for his authorship is detailed at some length
used by the author as a pseudonym
written primarily by... but issued under the signature of...
written under the allonym of...

ASSOCIATES

among her intimates were the likes of...
best remembered for his collaboration with...
he corresponded frequently with...
his harshest critic and most devoted friend
occasionally collaborated with...
the exact nature of their relationship is not known
was a schoolmate of...
was deeply involved with...
was intimately associated with...

AUTHORITY

a widely respected authority on...
contemporary authority on...
everyone can benefit from this veteran's wisdom and advice
one of the best authorities of the period
remained the principal authority on this subject until...
remarkable for his accurate knowledge of...
the foremost specialist on...
the standard authority on the subject
devoted herself to the study of...
devoted most of his career to...
gained practical experience as...
his early work brought him to the attention of...
his literary career began with the publication of...
marks a turning point in his career
the author has long experience in...
went on to a prolific career

CO-AUTHOR

also by...
...also had a hand in...
assembled by a brilliant cast of contributors
have teamed up to offer...
in conjunction with...
one of many who contributed to this work

their first book appearance together
...was the continuator of this work, begun by...
written in part if not entirely by...

CONTEMPORARIES

along with most of the important poets of his day
developed personal relationships with a variety of literary figures
had considerable influence over contemporaries
his ideas found a sounding board in...
influential among other writers
part of a circle of young liberals
under the warping influence of...
with whom he is often compared

FAILURE - LIFE

died a forgotten man
dissipation ruined him irrevocably
he began to drink excessively
he died disillusioned and anguished
he lived poor and out of favor
he was recklessly extravagant and died in want
his life fell to ruins about him
was a financial failure

FAILURE - WORK

an abortive attempt at producing a second book
fell with a dull thud
followed his predecessors into obscurity
his argument was widely discredited
his proposals proved impractical
overshadowed by...
sales of his first title were disappointing
she never fulfulled her early promise
the artistic quality of his work is not highly regarded
the book's reception brought little encouragement

FAME

a distinguished scholar well known for...
a hitherto unknown
a living legend
a well-known figure of the time
first achieved notoriety with...
found ready acceptance on the continent as well as at home
he is especially recognized for his...
justly famous
more well known than most
noted for both scholarship and elegance
particularly known for his delightful treatment of...
vaulted into prominence
well-known throughout literary circles of the day

FIRSTS

first book published under the author's own name
first major work by...
he did so well before anyone else thought to
his considerable talent is first seen in...
his first commercial book appearance
second book and first novel
the author's first and only book
the author's first attempt at this style
the author's first book on the subject of...
the first of his books to be translated
this book is usually considered his first for this press
this constitutes the first time his name appeared in print

IDEAS

a leading speculative thinker
a striking expression of the author's political views
an independent thinker
both... and... arrived at similar conclusions
generated much speculation
generous and expansive in his admiration of...
he concludes enthusiastically that...

he draws some troubling conclusions
he set out to explore...
he was the chief proponent of...
his arguments have merit
his point is soundly proven
his thoughtful opinions were held in the highest regard
offers his perceptive views on...
shows special insight
the argument offered suggests...
the scope of his ideas is astonishing
this volume invites speculation about...

INFLUENCE

has the power to preserve the past
he was in a preeminent position
he was instrumental in bringing the facts to light
he was keenly mindful of...
her idea was taken up with enthusiasm by...
his influence extended beyond the literary realm
his influence is not easily exaggerated
his influence is pervasive
his influence on American culture was incalculable
his influence was both wide and deep
his name carried weight among...
his work awakened interest in...
his work resulted in a gigantic leap in interest in the subject
pioneer of modern expression
sparked great interest in this vital subject
strongly influenced by...
swayed the public to believe...
the first to undermine conventional thinking

INNOVATION

ahead of his time
an innovative and dynamic participant
championed this idea before it became fashionable
didn't follow the dictates of...

foresaw the need
introduced the method of...
laid the groundwork
lead the way in contemporary issues
one of the earliest works to give an account of...
one of the seminal forerunners of...
paved the way for artistic expression
refused to run with the herd
remembered as the originator of the hypothesis that...
responsible for significant innovations
the first in a tradition which was to continue
the primary catalyst
this was the germinal idea which lead to...
truly a pioneer

LIFE PERIOD

a relatively early work
an explosive time in the life of...
at the peak of his career
born to easy privilege
early in his remarkable career
even at an early age he had a talent for lively writing
from his dramatically fruitful years
from the first year he published
his was a life fraught with change
it was here that he conceived and began work on...
made at the peak of ...'s powers
published shortly before his death
went through a period of deep depression
written at the height of his powers
written at the nadir of the author's reputation
written during his most intense and productive period of life
wrote during a time of great distress

LIFE'S WORK

a fascinating assessment of his work
a survey of his work shows that...

an important study by a prominent scholar of...
deserves to be one of his most acclaimed works
documents the author's preoccupation with...
found its finest realization in the work of...
he first became interested in...
he was a steady source of great books
he wrote a most influential book
her later accomplishments included...
her works were in the main humorous
his breakthrough book
his distinctive books are worthy of study
his fervent endeavor
his most famous character first appears in this volume
his penultimate work
his work will stand as the most comprehensive ever compiled
justly regarded as the most satisfying of his work
labored under a great handicap
little information is available on the life and works of...
made notable contributions
part of the legacy of his printed works
perhaps his first work of importance is...
produced many titles but this is the most noteworthy
the author's favorite among his own works is...
the driving force behind...
the last novel he was to publish
the last of his full-scale works
typical of his work
wrote the text personally

PERSONALITY

a curmudgeon and a misanthrope
an enlightened and intelligent woman
having a distinguished air
his temperament greatly contrasted with that of...
his was a nervous energy
not at all a critic by inclination
one of the more strident voices of the time

only one facet of this multi-faceted man
the range of his interests was enormous
was a flamboyant woman

POSTHUMOUS

chiefly remembered for...
gained immortality
his ideas have remained alive while others have passed
is exclusively remembered for...
little remembered since his death
more truly remembered as the author of...
no collection was published during her lifetime
particularly remembered for...
perhaps best remembered as...

PRAISE

a true scholar
an old master
by a great master of prose
by the incomparable...
demonstrates a degree of professionalism rarely seen
deserving of respect
further evidence of her special qualities as an observer
has a wonderful command of the language
he approaches a daunting subject fearlessly
his talent is at full throttle
most articulate
one of the most interesting commentators on the social scene
precocious
prodigiously talented
remarkably likeable and brilliant
representative of... at his best
shows profound knowledge
truly a giant in his field

REPUTATION

always spoken of with respect
better known for his steamy novels
by an amateur of eminence
considered to be not the best but the only authority on the subject
gained recognition
has a well established literary reputation
he acquired a world-class reputation
her reputation is upheld by such works as this
highly regarded for his innovative genius
his reputation over the years has been built on...
is best known today as an authority on...
known for his establishment of...
later became notorious as..
spoken of with respect
the author was in fact a ...
the basis for his reputation
this established his reputation
this novel enhanced his popularity and his literary reputation
widely credited with...
widely respected

SOURCE - PERSONAL

a most successful imitator
based largely on personal knowledge
being the result of nine years experience
capitalized on his success
contains much personal gossip
did much early exploratory work
discovered and gradually pieced together from...
drew heavily for inspiration
from perceptive observations
he committed to paper much oral history
he wrote it in almost the same words that he had heard
may have been patterned after...
may have been prompted by...
...'s most prominent desciple

the author was an eyewitness to events transpiring during...
the fruit of his work
the real-life prototype

SOURCE - SCHOLARLY

compiled from eyewitness accounts
compiled from primary sources
devoted himself to the study of...
his work shows considerable research
largely derived from...
made use of great historical records
virtually all his novels are based on fact
well-researched facts interspersed with personal observations

SUCCESS

a fairly productive hack novelist
a moderately successful playwright
among the most successful producers
at the top of his game
he came from humble origins to extraordinary eminence
he electrified the world of science with this work
he had the field almost entirely to himself
in this work, he realized the ambition of his literary career
saw his many projects reach fruition
was able to enjoy a happy idleness in his old age

SUPERLATIVES

a towering giant of 19th century Romanticism
author's most famous volume
by one of the best-known authors of the 1920s
he had no worthy successor
most prolific author in the field
noblest and most able
one of the greatest names in the history of...
one of the greats of all time

one of the most beloved writers of our time
the greatest living writer
the most brilliant of his day
written by the single most important figure in...

Prints

ABSTRACT

almost abstract quality
an example of artistic vision
fluent artistic style
is artsy
naive, original imagery
presents a visual mystique
stylized design
with a painterly sense of design

ACTION

a bright and lively scene
a visually exciting print which shows...
captures the excitement and pagaentry
contains scenes of the company in action
filled with information and exciting action
graphically captures a frenzy of activity
has a visual vitality all its own
possesses enormous charm and vivacity
set things in motion
this lively illustration depicts...
this rousing print well captures the drama of the scene

ARTIST - ACHIEVEMENTS

became one of the city's leading engravers
by an accomplished nineteenth century amateur
revolutionized the depiction of...

ARTIST - FAME

a celebrated early comedic artist
engraved by the well-known...

his distinct style is recognizable even without his signature
his prints are known for their bright attractive appearance
known for his drawings, engravings, and teaching
typically, he focused on inland waterways

ARTIST - IDENTIFICATION

color lithograph plate after watercolors by...
drypoints captioned and signed by the artist
engraver not identified
hand-colored engraved plates by and after the author
identified as being from the studio of...
the design for this is attributable to...
unattributed
with uncredited illustrations

ARTIST - SKILL

a fine example of...'s use of...
a generous artistic statement
a graphic milestone
an adroit rendering
captured the image with great dexterity
continually experimented with techniques and materials
exhibits the professional caliber that created his reputation
had an acute eye for detail
he took copious notes and made many sketches
his bird's eye views are noted for their superior quality
his skill enabled him to capture the image with great dexterity
inspired eye for detail
of considerable artistic value especially in light of the limitations of the medium
printed many of his own plates
produced by the most skilled etcher on the Continent
recorded by this highly skilled artist
shows artistic excellence
shows rare artistic talent
shows the considerable skill he brought to his craft
skillfully drawn, and altogether delightful

the most dramatic and well drawn
there are few prints that are its equal in quality of production
use of sunlight and shadow are very effective
versatile as well as prolific

ARTIST - STYLE

a fine example of...'s style
had an affinity for the primitive
had avant-garde artistic concepts
he continually experimented with techniques and materials

BACKGROUND

a picturesque setting with lush rural surroundings
a woodcut with diapered background
affords a distant glimpse of...
against a pale pink background
in a natural setting
nestled in the midst of a romanticized countryside
shown prominently on the far left is...
the background is incidental to the scene depicted
the physical surroundings lay quietly in the background
well depicted park-like setting
with a natural scenic background

BORDERS

a typical flower entwined border
closely cropped lower border barely affecting part of neat line
delightful border vignettes
elaborate border enlivened with imaginary scenes
fluted corners provide balance and elegance
framed in an elaborate array of angels, cherubs and filigree
in an elaborate architectural border
printed within wide, lushly foliated borders
set in a rope and banner framework
surrounded by an ornate border
with varicolored floral and animal motifs
with wide ornamental borders

within a ruled frame
within cleverly designed borders
within fancy frames
within interlocking scrolls

BOTANICALS - COLOR

colorful clusters of blooms
filled with colorful blossoms and leaves
multicolored specimen
pastel florets
unusually colorful

BOTANICALS - FLOWERS

abundant flowers of rich shades
bell-shaped on spike
borne on long stems
clustered blossoms
dainty flowers
daisy-shaped flowers
distinguished by great size of individual flowers
globe-shaped flower heads
goblet shaped blooms
large delicate reddish cluster
lush, frilly bloom
on stately spikes
outstanding for the quality of blossoms
pendulous flowers
showy blossoms
stunning yellow centers
wide open blooms
with extravagant blossoms

BOTANICALS - FOLIAGE

carefully arranged, stylized leaves
clearly defined edging
deeply incised
diminutive variety

distinctive horizontal branching
elongated, twisted segments
emphasizes the upward flow with graceful lines
fantastically twisted and turned
feathery, fernlike texture
glistening green foliage
glossy arrow shaped leaves
graceful leaves complement impressive blooms
lance shaped leaves
leathery texture of deep green leaves
stems float upward in graceful curves
stunning display of rich, green foliage
unusual weeping habit
waxy compound leaves
with sinuous foliage designs

BOTANICALS - PETALS

delicately ruffled petals
glowing apricot edges
overlapping petals
ruffled, fluted petals
satiny purple petals
translucent petals
vivid red petals

BOTANICALS - PRAISE

a direct imitation from nature
a favorite subject among botanical illustrators
admirably suggests the lushness of a tropical paradise
an opulent display
beautiful and graceful
creates a marvelous contrast
exotic, long treasured species
garden beauty
lovely blooms against decorative foliage

ornamental elegance
spectacular display
truly the showiest

BOTANICALS - SCIENTIFIC

each flower is identified by its scientific name
images are botanically correct
listed by common name in use at the time
new to science
obsolete Latin name

BUILDINGS

a church steeple rises above the infant town
depicted in the distance are several other identifiable buildings
nine buildings shown but only three identified
pedestrians and carriages are depicted but the main empahasis is on the building
shown here as it was remodeled in...
shows the building soon after it was built
sites are easily identifiable
the building depicted still stands and now serves as...
the building is shown in a forested setting
the impressive size of the building is highlighted by the milling figures around its base

BUILDINGS - EXTINCT

depicts the original structure before it was rebuilt
many of the structures depicted are no longer standing
the structure depicted burned down in...
this print gives us an intimate idea of how the building was used then
this striking edifice burned in spectacular fashion
this view is intended to show the structure as it stood in the eighteenth century
very few printed images of the site exist

BUILDINGS - PRAISE

a clear rendering of the buildings
a lovely classical building
a precise image of the building
an impressive structure due to its imposing size and construction
the buildings are drawn with excellent accuracy
the image is one of the more impressive ever published of this building
this image illustrates how gracefully the building is flanked by two wings

BUILDINGS - STYLE

careful attention to architectural details
expresses the aesthetics of architecture
large Victorian affair
striking gothic edifice
with ornately carved wrap-around porches

CITIES

a document of the soul of the city
a rich image of the city and its watery surroundings
a splendid view of a vibrant and confident city
an excellent reference source of the city from the end of the century
captured the feeling of life in the city
clearly the region's transportation center
gives us a special glimpse of the city and its people
one of the earliest American city views
probably the earliest extant view of the city
provides us with the best image obtainable of the city at that period
providing an unusual example of the iconography of the city
shown in its prosaic workday reality
shows almost the entire extent of the city
the city is depicted as a busy seaport
the city stands in the background with smoke pouring from two buildings
the highlight of a wonderful corpus illustrating the city
the thriving business community is well documented here
with smoke stacks billowing around the city and in the distance

CITY STREETS

a good-natured street scene
conveys a sense of the lively, bustling activity of the street
each structure along the street is precisely depicted
one of the most delightful street tableaux ever done
picturesque small city of quiet shady streets
streets and major buildings are depicted and named
successfully captures the street life
the scene is bustling with pedestrian and vehicular activity
vivid, lively street scene

CITY'S GROWTH

a growing modern urban center
accurately and exquisitely chronicles the city's growth
documents the changing landscape of the city
emphasizes burgeoning commerce and industry
growing industrialization is documented
part of a fascinating story of the city's development
perhaps the finest contemporary document of the city's new appearance
preserving a city soon to change
progressed toward becoming a modern metropolis
shows the city poised to enter the new century

CLUTTERED

cluttered and overly complex
cluttered and inelegant
ornate and fussy
overdone, laden with extraneous decoration
overwhelming elaborate decoration
precisely places numerous small designs

COMPARISON

appears more like an original watercolor than a print
has much of the naive charm of folk art
has the appearance of watercolor

somewhat more decorative
the projected plan illustrated is very different from the one finally adopted

COMPOSITION

a tree stands majestically in the center
centers on a dramatic incident
entirely encompassed in a single panoramic view
in a recurrent pattern
in the foreground..., while further back...
in vertical format
included as an inconspicuous foreground feature
posed like wooden soldiers
prominently positioned in the lower center of the print
slightly to the right of center is...
somewhat unconventional composition
the composition and design are pleasing
the main image is surrounded by many smaller views
unusual composite
with a dramatic central subject
with a wealth of foreground detail
with the skyline much compressed

COMPOSITION - PRAISE

a well rendered scene
design flows harmoniously from front to back
making artistic use of narrow space
masterful composition
poetically composed
the composition is dramatic and the detail excellent
the detail and composition is excellent

CONTENT

a finely drawn domestic scene
a montage of views of...
a most unusual interior view of...
a prominent feature was...

an allegorical scene representing...
an appealing scene
the dramatic event depicted is...
the subject matter was wide ranging

CRITICISM

example of a lack of concern with correct images
produced an impersonal effect
uninspired though competent rendering

DECORATIVE

a most striking decorative format
a very pleasing picture
adding to the attractiveness of this particular item
an impressive piece, perfect to frame
arrives at a striking effect
both color and form are agreeable in design
displays flair
dramatically displays
exceptionally decorative item
immensely pleasing drawings
often graced private homes and public buildings
presented in a superb format
spectacular piece to hang on a wall
uniquely decorative
utilitarian and decorative
you'll want to display this one

DETAIL

a human document that preserves many small, meaningful details
a magnifying glass will help
a rich array of realistic decorative details
a well composed, highly detailed drawing
attention to fine detail as well as the overall picture
full of charming primitve details
full of deftly arranged details
it is impressive how much of the detail has been preserved

meticulously detailed image
one of the many interesting aspects of this print
rendered in loving detail
two features of note are...
with parsimonious lack of detail

EDITION - EARLY

a fine set of engraving proofs before letters
a fresh, early impression
annotated artist's proof
many are early proofs
progressive proofs of the lithographs
the first edition to document...
the first etchings pulled from these plates
the first generally available version
with its deckled edge and excellent impression, it is likely a sample pull

EDITION - LATER

a completely new stone was drawn and many details added
a late impression from a worn plate
altered from the originals
an updated edition of...'s view
apparently a later printing or from worn plates
appears identical to first edition
continued to be reissued over quite some years
from the same plate as the earlier edition
issued in new editions almost annually
it is a reduction of the earlier version
later, reengraved edition
reissued several times and copied by other publishers
repeated virtually unchanged on subsequent copies
restrike from the original plate
the basic features remain unchanged in subsequent editions
third hand from the original
updated an earlier plate of unknown origin

EDITION - SIGNED

inscribed in the stone lower center
signed and dated in brush
signed and titled in pencil
signed by the artist and inscribed in another hand
signed in ink by the artist and the sitter
signed in the stone
the artist is identified only by his initials

EDITION - SIZE

edition of one hundred or less
edition size probably small
edition unknown, presumably very small
in limited editions of unknown size
issued in six fascicles of four prints each
one of a small number of pulls
only twelve of the intended twenty-six prints were produced
probable edition of one hundred

EDITION - STATE

an extremely rare first state of this image
in proof state
probably an engraver's proof
second state of two
second state with retouching and stamped signature added
the third of four equally uncommon editions
third plate, fourth state
third state, with added seagulls
this state is identical to the first
with the plates in four states, one being in color

EDITION - OTHER

contemporaneous editions
portfolio edition
the history of this edition of the engraving is unclear
this desirable print was separately issued

EMOTIONAL

a beautiful, highly romantic vision
a deeply disturbing look at...
a melodramatic view
a reflection of the romantic concepts of the day
emotionally charged scene
evokes a mood of enchantment
excited patriotic fervor
expresses the mood of...
generates an intense emotional response
gently sentimental
gives a feeling of vibrancy
highly dramatic rendering
lending a feeling of serenity
melodramatic content

EXECUTION

an unfinished "ghost print"
engraved plates printed back to back
printed from the original litho plates
printed from two copper plates
printed in color and finished by hand
printed slowly on hand made paper
with barely perceptible printing block seams
with clearly visible facet edges
with countless fine lines

EXECUTION - PRAISE

a good rich printing
beautiful dark impression
carefully and elegantly rendered
carefully colored
clean, dark impression
clear and readable
excellent delineation of textures
executed with great care
expertly rendered and attractively colored

fine execution
finely drawn
firm, well-inked impressions
image is sharp, bright and clean
reasonably strong image
registration of various color tones is perfect
reproduced with astonishing fidelity
strong, attractively colored impression
superb technique
superbly reproduced
technically and aesthetically excellent
technically sophisticated engraving
technically surpasses most work done to date
the registration is very exact
the subject is well realized
very vivid, sharp, clean image
with image generally strong and clear

FASHION

conveys information on the dress and manners of the city dwellers
faces, movements and clothes are rendered in loving detail
their formal dress and manners are graphically illustrated

FAULTS

bleeds to the edge
imperfectly executed
relatively crude
slightly out of register
small area of stain from printing plate
smudged in a couple of places
the erasure was only partly successful
the print shows a light ghost image
with some streaking

FIGURES

a small figure set off-center attempts to liven the scene
accented by a solitary figure

an added element of interest is the many strollers passing by
bizarre figures are depicted
elegant couples promenade through
figure was crudely engraved and quite out of scale
figures are stiff and awkward
human figures are drawn convincingly
idealized figures
many of the figures shown are identifiable notables
natural poses
showing a solitary form
straight and precise as wooden soldiers
the figures add interest to the scene
the human figures are particularly well rendered
the pedestrians and workmen add interest to the scene
unfinished, with some figures having no shading
with a solitary figure standing on the shore

FOLDS

folds into two sections as intended for practical use
neatly folded
vertical printer's crease
with the usual center paper fold
with vertical centerfold

FOLDS - REPAIRED

centerfold entirely reinforced on verso
centerfold separation repaired
fold crudely repaired obscuring image
half-inch lower centerfold separation repaired on verso
margin part of lower centerfold repaired

FRAMES

apparently in good condition, not examined out of frame
archival framing under ultra violet glass
laid down on board and framed

mounted with gum adhesive between glass
nicely framed
the frame is part of the artwork

HISTORICAL

a cheerful print with no evidence of the tragedy to follow
a visual chronicle of the event
depicts episodes of discovery and exploration
depicts historical figures and events
more concern for factual detail than technique
pretentious historical composition
reflects the historic approach to this important site
satisfied a great interest in the history of the region
this print reflects the historical approach to this important site

LANDSCAPES

a dazzling, sunny view
a rather desolate view
a rhythmic landscape
a scene of untamed wilderness
a trail through the brush and swamp
a tranquil, primeval scene
admirably suggests a vast landscape
an unspoiled landscape setting
created an artificial, romantic landscape
dense woodland foliage and jumbled rock formations
expansive skies above green pastures
illustrating the layout of the land
in this picturesque setting
pastoral scene in foreground
preserves an early, undisturbed landscape
rather stark, gloomy scene
set in landscaped grounds with fountains and winding paths
suggests the vast extent of a magnificent spectacle
the sky suggests a passing storm
view of an unspoiled and natural land
with sweeping atmospheric effects

LANDSCAPES AND MAN

a superb blending of natural beauty enhanced by man's technological mastery
dramatic conflict between man and the elements
represents the interaction between man and nature
unspoiled by human activity
appropriately matted

MATS

dimensions as visible under mat
fully custom conservation matted
hinged to mat with printed captions
mounted to stiff mat with ample margins
mounted with wide margins to publisher's decorative mat
properly matted
some mat burn
very mild mat burn and foxing

MILITARY

a detailed and informative look at an important battle
a representation of the conflict between America and Great Britain
an unsurpassed reflection of the tense moments of war
depicts the battle which created a military hero
documented the events and scenes of the war
fort dominates view of...
from sketches drawn on the battlefield
provided the public with current and accurate pictures of the war
the terrible face of war as it appeared to those who viewed it

MONUMENTS

a fine view of this proud centerpiece of the city
created to memorialize the Civil War
impressive size in contrast to tiny figures shown at the base
lovely view of this important structure
one of the most desirable images of this important landmark
shows the monument in its original park setting

standing proudly on a carved pedestal
stands out like a showpiece
with crowds strolling around the base of the structure

MOUNTED

laid down onto board
mounted on linen for durability
mounted on textured, beveled board
tipped to a mount
tipped to a sheet on which is stamped...
window mounted

NAUTICAL

a plethora of sailing vessels in the river and tied to the piers
a small sailing vessel lends a sense of serenity to the image
adapted for maritime traffic
decorated with numerous sailing ships
motionless sailboats and a vast expanse of sky
shows crew racing on the river
swarming with ships of all sorts
the nautical interest is greater than the topographical
with a veritable flotilla of ships in the sea

PERSPECTIVE

a "horizontorium" which can be seen with normal perspective only when viewed at an angle
a mile-long panorama
a most unusual perspective view of...
drawn from an imaginary perspective
from a purely imaginative viewpoint
from a rooftop vantage point that provides a spectacular view
oblique panorama
seen from across the river banks
seen in the distance beneath the tree's branches
slightly to the right of center stands...
taken from an extremely elevated view point
the buildings are put into perspective by the depiction of...

the city proper can be seen in the distance past the bridge
the image centers on...
the perspective looks west towards...
the view is oriented to look up the river
this vantage point was used for a number of paintings of...
with atmospheric depth

PERSPECTIVE - PRAISE

an excellent bird's eye view of...
perspective is convincingly rendered
rendered with attention to space and clarity
with the graceful generalities of a panoramic view

PHOTOGRAPHER

from original negative under photographer's supervision
imprinted with photographer and date printed on reverse
remembered for his faithful pictures of a vanishing world
signed and captioned in the negative
special edition initialed by photographer
with photographer's hand-stamp on the reverse side

PORTRAITS

believed to be the most satisfactory likeness
formal, chest-length study
photographic portrait plates in collotype
posed in the studio in full uniform
three-quarter-length seated portrait

PRAISE

a noteworthy view
a particularly elegant view
a rich and varied group of images
among its visual delights... are included
an imaginative expression of a way of life
an intimate closely observed scene
an unsurpassed pictorial record
captured an old picturesque charm

delicate depiction
depicts the great natural beauty of...
impeccable little print
provides a delightful look at...
the overall effect is quite pleasant
the plates are as fresh as the day they were published
this vibrant view

PRESENTATION

cased images
consists of three panels side by side
illustration on verso of songsheet
in the original presentation folder
inlaid into slightly larger sheet
loosely gathered into paper sleeve
loosely laid into lightly worn pictorial jacket
original fascicles with paper covers
printed in reverse
printed on one side of folded sheets
printed on rectos only
the verso also has imagery
this song sheet cover was not printed in any other format

PURPOSE

print was used as a promotional gift
produced to grace the cover of...
the prints were intended to be sold very inexpensively
these prints were produced for very different reasons
this print is an illustrated membership certificate
this sensational print was issued to commemorate...
this separately issued print was published as a souvenir
to provide us with a wide ranging view

REALISM

accurately drawn
carefully constructed images
drawn with controlled exuberance

injected a harsh realism
labored image
mastery of form and nuances of color
presented a far greater truth
realistic, skillfully drawn animals in delightful settings
recorded with eyewitness precision
rendered with a realistic immediacy
with uncanny realism

RURAL

a delightful microcosm of town and country
picturesquely rural
portrays rustic, rural charm
showing layout of town and surrounding area
shows cottages in the immediately surrounding countryside
shows the structure in a rural setting
spared the development that marked other places
sparse settlement in the area is evident
spread well beyond the city limits
studded with homes
the apparently rural location was soon to see rapid development
the bucolic setting is evident from the grazing cows
with each town and many roads shown

SERIES

a series of sketches
here are three color prints of the same image
progressively reflects more details
shows a nice sequence of growth
this set of four prints combines to form a panoramic view of...
wood-engravings which are all printed from the original blocks

SIZE

a large folio print
an unusually small engraving that contains interesting details
occupying a full page
platework size varies

SOURCE

an exceptional page from...
edges trimmed (probably removed from a bound volume)
many of the illustrations were taken from other sources
originally published in...

SOURCE - CONTENT

a print perhaps inspired by...
a small and rare derivative of...
after designs by...
after original photographic views
based on plans and drawn prior to the actual event
his last painting to be made into a print
original drawing from which he made this engraving
renderings taken from plans
taken from an on-the-spot drawing made by a staff illustrator
the images for the prints were taken from official plans
these views were taken from previously issued larger views
this view is closely derived from...'s earlier image
though hypothetical, this print has a basis in fact
used...'s images, which he published without attribution

STYLE

a native flavor provides a part of its appeal
a new dramatic graphic form
as if swept by the wind
brooding, atmospheric etchings
dark, rather ominous scene
formal images
freely rendered drawing
in a scattered, swirling design
intense, powerful designs
naive but appealing
of oriental flavor
of striking quality
possesses rugged charm
producing an overall charming effect

rigid, segmented look
slightly primitive character
the lure of this print is...
unmistakably symbolic
with a professional flair

TEXT

attractively captioned in a contemporary hand
beneath the image is listed a roster
hand written decoration
photographs are identified in pencilled captions
printed with a letterpress
the scene has a key printed below the image
with supporting sheet

TOPOGRAPHY

bold and mountainous
broad plains richly verdant
craggy ravines and bleak moors
hills and sloping vales
rocky and precipitous coast

TYPE - COLOR

aquatint, chiaroscuro, chromolithograph, chromoxylograph, chromotypograph, duotone, tinted
a woodcut with the image printed in four shades of green
hand colored via the stencil process
illustrations colored through pochoir
lithographed in two colors

TYPE - ENGRAVINGS

collagraph, copper, dotted, drypoint, etching, line block, linocut, metalcut, mezzotint, steel, soft ground, stipple
a dark and potent woodcut
a commanding and vigorous engraving
a white-line wood engraving

TYPE - PHOTOGRAPHS

albumen, ambrotype, collotype, daguerrotype, halftone
chromolithograph, lithograph, screenprint,
instantaneous motion photographs
photo-collage offset lithograph in colors
photographic print in blue-tones
photogravure printed in sepia
reproduced by photo-mechanical process
snapshots of personal subjects
toned silver prints of copy negatives
with white ink annotations on the image

TYPE - PRAISE

efficient and inexpensive medium
an exceptionally fine example of nature printing
high quality black and white lithographs with tonal subtleties
important early example of the use of lithography
one of the first lithographic views made of the city
photographs of remarkable definition and clarity
represents the first great period of lithography
the best and clearest form of reproduction
the engravings are immensely pleasing
visually beautiful and finely engraved
visually strong miniature woodcuts

WATER

admirably conveys the overwhelming force of the falling water
conveys the charm of a rural stream
dramatic play of light and shade in sea and sky
portrays treacherous shoals
serene, mirror smooth harbor

Maps

ACCURACIES

drawn presumably with great accuracy
nothing of its kind matches its accuracy and thoroughness
one of the most accurate
published after more information was available and therefore more accurate
quite a bit of information, most of it relatively accurate
rather accurately drawn
shown with commendable accuracy
shows a strikingly accurate representation of...
shows the current knowledge of its shape, size and contours
the earliest map with any claims to accuracy
the most accurate map then available

ADDITIONS

an exact copy except for the addition of...
an expanded chart
considerably updated from the original issue of six years earlier
extensively revised to include a more fully defined outline
has significant additions
minor changes were made in 18.., the imprint date
presented new details on the tributaries of the... River
presents little new geographical information
reissued here in an updated version
scores of new towns added
shows states recently carved out of the Northwest Territory
the woodblock for this map was considerably updated from the original issue
with added road and town information
with changes mostly in the embellishments
with some updating

AREA SHOWN - CENTRAL

approximately bisected by the Mississippi River
centers on the area between... and...
centrally located
covers area for 10 miles on either side of...
primarily illustrates Africa
showing a ten mile radius around the city
showing original semi-circular layout of the city
the highlight of this well executed map is...
the map focuses on the center city area

AREA SHOWN - EASTERN

all of the east coast except Florida
confined to the east coast
covers the colonies and extends across Appalachia
from Philadelphia to Maine
region of the original thirteen colonies
the eastern coastline

AREA SHOWN - WESTERN

a decorative map showing west to Missouri Territory
and then continuing northwest to incorporate the vast Terra Incognita
delineation of areas west of the Mississippi is speculative
extended west toward...
extending indefinitely westward
extends west to include...
map of the west as it was for only a short time
settlements get thin in the north and west
shows the western extremity of...
shows to the... (Pacific)
the most westerly part of the state
to the far west is...
vast areas in the west with no political development

AREA SHOWN - OTHER

appears almost exactly on the site of modern day...
Asia is there on the right side of the map sheet

basically, the map covers the north half of the state
covers the area between 25 and 35 degrees
encompasses the entire known land mass of the New World
extending well into what is now...
extends to the... and just beyond
in close proximity to...
map of... from... to just past
perhaps the most significant feature is the appearance of...
providing excellent coverage of...
shows almost the entire extent of the city
shows eastern half of...
shows only areas definitely verified
shows the extreme limits of...
shows the immediately surrounding countryside
shows... and somewhat beyond
somewhat more remote
stretches from... to...
the map extends slightly further than...
this map lays emphasis on the waterfront
this map shows an area now in..., along the Hudson
this sheet includes the site of...

BOUNDARIES

a red line has been drawn to mark the boundary between...
boundaries as they are today save for...
divided into six mile square townships
each state shown with its final boundaries
identifies boundaries by natural landmarks
map of the area bounded by...
no boundary line between... and... shown
notable for its sweeping vertical boundaries
shown without a northern border
the boundaries are nothing like those of today
this boundary was actually fixed further north
updated to show the new boundaries between...
with a large irregular dip in the boundary line

with clearly defined boundaries
with its original boundaries taking a chunk out of...
with probable boundaries of...

CARTOUCHE

a bright copy with a decorative cartouche
a large distinctive cartouche showing natives, animals and birds
a major feature is the large, exceptionally decorative uncolored cartouche
an accurately engraved beaver surmounts a decorative cartouche
banner cartouche with cherubs
boasts a flamboyantly executed title
crowded with people and products characteristic of the place
exceptionally attractive pictorial title cartouche
features two lavishly decorative cartouches
Indians in native dress add atmosphere to the cartouche
large ornate strapwork title cartouche
ornate title cartouche
plain title cartouche
reminiscent of Mercator's style and possibly a homage to him
the effect is heightened by the swash lettering
the elaborate cartouche interweaves figures, foliage and treasure
title cartouche inexplicably includes a...
title in drapery cartouche
with costumed figures in a fretwork cartouche
with vignettes of indigenous flora and fauna

COASTAL CHARTS

a portolan of the coast of...
a series of charts, with sailing directions
accompanied by a finely drawn coastal view
channels through tricky waters are carefully plotted
defines a secure haven sheltered by islands
gives depth readings for...
has the rhumb lines of a sea chart
intended to be used as a navigational aid for ships sailing toward...
popular with the armchair sailor

primarily a sea chart having rhumb lines and a compass rose
shows a great accuracy of soundings
shows the principal port of maritime activity
shows the shape of the land in profile
the 'Bible' to navigators in that period
the main shipping lane is indicated with depths marked
thirty copies of this chart were distributed to naval officers
truly useful for navigation
with coastal and inland detail
worn out from use at sea

COLOR

a lovely example of two-color cartographic printing
brightly colored by wards
colorful, informative map of the...
colors are by geological strata
each ward is colored in a contrasting pastel shade
fine bright color by county
full body color along..., outline color along...
full color by state
major buildings are shown highlighted in white
outline and some wash color accentuate the boundaries
this is a clear, colorful map
with colored boundary lines
with two separately colored blank areas

COMPARISON

best map of the area available
covers a wider area than is usually depicted
differing in title, size and plate number
markedly superior to previous works showing this area
one of the better maps showing...
provided more information about the area than any other map of the period
published, unchanged from map first drawn in 18....
shows the same essential information as... but includes...

CONTENT

a distributional map of...
clear depiction of the major trails of the west
depicting precisely the locale of...
detailed map showing placement of...
Indian country with many tribes named
interesting for what it shows, what it omits and what has changed
notable for its content and for its format
particularly interesting for the depiction of the western territories
scattered throughout is the simple label 'gold'
shows economical features such as timber, grazing and arid lands
shows historically interesting points such as...
shows the contemporary layout of the city
streets and major buildings are depicted and named
the map includes a depiction of a projected plan for...

CORRECTIONS

a marked improvement in detail and accuracy
by 1800 maps of this region had assumed a modern look
clarified the shape of...
corrected an earlier misconception
corrected many cartographical errors
dramatically updated the cartography of...
has been correctly changed to...
in revised form with some changes
quickly followed by a second corrected edition
reprinted with minor corrections
shows basic improvements in the shape of...
the excesssive width of the sea has been narrowed
the most correct map of the area yet to appear
this area was scantily and inaccurately portrayed on earlier maps

DECORATIVE

art as well as geography
charming decorative elements grace the map
decorated with vignettes of inhabitants and domestic scenes
disguised ignorance with decoration

embellished with heraldic crests, sea monsters, and sailing ships
in addition to its decorative qualities, it captures a moment in history
includes vignettes of American cities
inscriptions on the map represent significant events
one of the great decorative maps in the history of cartography
sea monsters prowl the oceans
vivid scenes show the various signs of the zodiac
with full baroque ornamentation

DETAIL

a detailed map by any standard
a most comprehensive cartographic picture
contains many details sought by map users
copious details include property owners, toll booths, and mills
remarkable detail throughout
shows details which do not appear on other period maps
these details give us a wealth of information about...

DEVELOPMENT

a contemporary view of the region and its development
a pictorial chronicle of a swiftly changing scene
acres of reclaimed land transformed the shape of...
an invaluable record of early development
by 1800 this area assumed a modern look
communities dot the fringes
demonstrates the great open space of the state
depicts the growth of...
developed parts are indicated with shading while proposed streets are noted by dotted lines
early layout of towns is largely undeveloped
evidence of settlers incursion
has a statistical table of population
level of development is evident in number and distribution of counties
many modern cities are missing
many towns and settlements appear along the coast
new developments commanded the attention of cartographers
proposed streets are noted by dotted lines

recorded a rapidly changing and evolving state
recorded the opening of the frontier
records the newly emerging counties, towns and railroads
reflects the rapidly changing appearance of the city
showing signs of becoming...
shows the great influx of settlers
shows the humble beginnings of...
sparse settlement is evident
testifies to the rapid colonization of areas along the river
transformed into a habitable area
was a natural center for development
with no settlements between embryonic Chicago and Denver

DISCOVERIES

demonstrates the mapmaker's awareness of the most current information
filled in the details of the interior
gave recognizable shape to the coast of...
illustrates the expansion of geographical knowledge during the preceding years
just recently discovered
made familiar by successive explorations
now recognizable
produced with the aid of first hand scientific information
records for the first time the discoveries of...
shows the alleged discoveries of...
shows the area in a period of early discovery
shows the purported discoveries as indicated by...
tracing the cartographic history of...
well known and comparatively well mapped

DISTORTIONS

a very distended coast
an elongated east west outgrowth
best known for its gross distortion of features
bulges westward doubling its actual extent
contains the novelty of a jutting peninsula off the coast

fanciful shape
fantasy-like delineation
Great Lakes appear but are still misshapen
improperly drawn
mountain ranges seem to drift haphazardly across the land
naively delineated
oddly compressed
peculiar, top-heavy exaggeration
peninsula is somewhat misshaped
quite recognizable but somewhat distorted
somewhat distorted
squeezed New England in almost as an afterthought
still depicts the old westerly bulge
the configuration suggests that mapmakers were uncertain of its geography
the islands remain but are much reduced
the key distortion is...
the region appears too narrow
wishful thinking created the bizarre shape of...

EDITION

the Indian path appears exclusively in this edition
virtually identical to the mother map

EXPLORATION

accurately shows the tracks of...
communicated discoveries made in exploring...
explorations clarified the geography of the area
from the time when exploration was a government activity
on this map can be found the tracks and stopping points of...
published at a time of active exploration
routes of early explorers are traced with surprising accuracy
shows the tracks and stopping points of famous voyages
the first description of Hawaii after Cook
the first map marking the route of...
the tracks of... epic voyage are shown

IMPORTANCE

a cornerstone map of...
a foundation map
adding to the significance of this particular map
an epochal map
an influential image
became the official map used by the Post Office
definitely a key map of...
...depiction was accepted throughout Europe
determined the shape of the American landscape
exerted a profound influence on the delineation of the continent
historically and geographically significant
important because it is one of the last maps to show...
important for its early depiction of...
its greatest contribution was the mapping of the interior
maps of this region were a necessity
much else of interest and significance on this important map
one of the classic maps of...
part of an emerging cartographic record
part of the history of cartographic technology
provided the image many people had of...
reproduced by at least a half dozen map publishers
the earliest appearance on a printed map
the first dated map to show...
the first printed map to show...
the great contribution of this map lies in the depiction of...
the model for the delineation of... for thirty years
the most significant general map of this period
the prototype for other editions
this version had the widest dissemination
transitional map

INACCURACIES

almost correct but still looks a little odd
among the map's cartographic curiosities is...
an area where there was much geographic confusion
an erroneous look at the unknown interior of the continent

an error due to the inability to calculate longitude
an important map despite its inaccuracies
appealing in its absurdity
based on little firm knowledge
completely conjectural
completely fictitious placement of the river
contorted geography to comply with explorers' reports
copied on later maps for many years causing general confusion
depicted in elaborate if not accurate detail
dominated by this dramatic geographic misconception
enters the Great Salt Lake too far south
exhibits the peculiarity of an incompletely charted land mass
geographical information is only of antiquarian interest
highly inaccurate as is to be expected at this time
illustrates a notable geographic misconception
improbable mountains scattered across the landscape
known for its highly imaginative delineation of...
largely blank and what does appear is inaccurate
later became a geographical monstrosity
nonexistent waterways
portrayed as being in the present latitude of...
portrays an enormous fictitious sea
reasonably correct for its time
reasonably if not accurately mapped
seriously misplaced too near...
several highly fanciful features make this unusual
shown in a near final configuration
situated far to the west of its actual location
supposed discoveries
surmises the existence of...
surprisingly inaccurate illustrations of...
the configuration is largely imaginary
the conjectured course of the river is marked with a dotted line
this imaginary mountain range reappeared for many years
uncertain as to whether it depicts.. or...
unrecognizable island
where geographical information was scanty and inaccurate

INSETS

an inset gives a key to the city wards
around the image are examples of...
enhanced by a pretty inset
inset views were added around the main image
insets embellish the lower corners
surrounding the map are insets of...
the insets add a great deal
the inset is the earliest published view of...
the inset is particularly fascinating as it shows...
the smaller insets are also valuable works
two insets grace the corners

MAPMAKER'S SKILL

assembled a wealth of information hitherto unavailable
became America's dominant cartographer
demonstrated the inadequacies of previous maps
greatest map publisher
his most successful cartographic publication
learned his craft from...
noted for a high degree of originality and accuracy
noted for excellence in mapmaking
one of the foremost cartographers of his time
one of the real triumphs of Dutch cartography
respected as a commercial publisher and scientific geographer
shows the considerable skill... brought to his craft
small, elegantly engraved maps designed by...
the first major cartographer to do so
the foremost publisher of maps used by...
the map is a good example of his exellent detail
the then leading mapmaker
unequalled for thoroughness and method

MAPMAKER'S SOURCE

a derivative
a finely detailed map copied from...
a small and rare derivative of...

based on a much larger map
based on independent sources and therefore unlike his contemporaries
carefully reduced from a larger map by...
copied by mapmakers for many years thereafter
drawn from the best authorities
he relied on a map prepared by...
mother map
one of the key maps used by...
probably based on...
probably copied from...
protoype of most maps of this section
relied on earlier surveys for the settled part of his map
the basis for many later maps
the engraver has incorporated features of several source maps
the prototype for the next twenty years
used a prototype

MILITARY

a contemporary plan of a decisive seige
a Revolutionary War-era map used by both British and American forces
depicts the troop movements of both sides
documents elements important to the outcome of battle
forts are scattered throughout the area
generally available to military strategists
include extensive historical information on troop movements
locates the city's formidable fortifications
many forts important during the war are indicated
meticulous attention to military strategies
provides a detailed depiction of troop movements
they got their victory in the engagement shown on this map
vivid cartographical record of the battle

MYTH

based on mythical discoveries
exhibits medieval geographical theories
illustrates the prevailing belief in the northwest passage

mmersed in a fog of myth
perpetuated the traditional belief that...
the mythical was replaced by fact after the discovery of...

OMISSIONS

blank instead of being filled with...
blank spaces are labled unexplored
geographical information is spotty
... is not represented at all
no hint of... nor would their be for another fifty years
omitted what he did not know firsthand
the interior is largely blank
untitled map of...
wisely left blank what was unknown

ORIENTATION

Boston is at upper left
direction is indicated by small north pointing arrows
ornate compass rose
separate maps with no common orientation
the charm lies in the orientation
the orientation is confusing
the orientation provides the most efficient use of space
the orientation of the map is to the west

PLACENAMES

accurately delineated but unnamed
considerably more placenames than the forerunner
crowded with placenames
depicting area which will become...
has a curious nomenclature
important for the inclusion of many names not appearing on other maps
in the middle of what was otherwise known as...
later to become...
major sites are carefully illustrated and named
many places noted but not identified
mythical placenames

named for the explorer who reported it
notable for a profusion of now defunct town names
notable for its profusion of names now lost to history
one of the earliest appearances of a name that would become
commonly used
quite a few placenames that no longer appear on modern maps
shows several archaic placenames
strange or now extinct placenames appear
the first published plan to name...
these streets were renamed in the last half of the century
which is thought to represent...
with a multitude of placenames
with a partially delineated, but clearly named...
with all place names in Italian

POCKET

bound into small, stiff covers
case contains ads for other maps
designed for easy portability
designed to fold into covers
folds into a buckram cover for portability
in a case which is worn at hinge but not split
limited to the manageable size demanded for a driving map

PRAISE

a superior rendering of this region
a very handsome and informative work
adding to the desirability of this map is...
beautifully combines science and decoration
excellent balance between embellishments and map
one of the masterworks of map printing
this monumental work was the first to show...
this spectacular and important map is also of great rarity
devoid of any political entities
giant counties predominate indicating sparse settlement
includes a projected plan for the forthcoming development
large, modern towns are missing

many of today's counties don't appear
shows a scene very different from the plan actually adapted
there is a large undivided area now occupied with several counties

PREDEVELOPMENT

already out of date by 1800
depicted the world on the eve of...
scrolls decoratively placed to obscure the unknown
the unknown territory has been hidden by an inset of...
these parts were little known
undreamed of

PREEXPLORATION

a pre-Cook conception of the coast
basically unexplored
little known and poorly mapped
much charting is yet to be done
tentatively drawn
the lands were imperfectly known
the most accurate available at the time
unimagined by its first explorers
was willing to leave unknown regions blank

PURPOSE

a fine example of an early "driving map"
absolutely indispensable map for...
an aid to those considering emigration
an index map is provided to facilitate use of the atlas
clearly presents information on roads and railroads that would be useful to the traveler
consulted in the arbitration of boundary disputes
documented property ownership
informative both cartographically and demographically
issued to illustrate a book
printed to accompany the official government report
separately issued wall map

RAILROADS

a clear view of the existing and planned networks
a web of railroads connects the cities and towns
bold red lines are punctuated by white lines indicating whistlestops
excellent coverage of early railroads
filled with scores of towns along the railroads
railroads traverse the entire state
roads linked with trains to form an interior network
shows better roads and an expanding railroad network
shows each small station and little else
shows more than fifty miles of railroad lines
shows railroads finished or in progress
shows roads with a spur in each direction
the transportation nexus is well depicted
with several spurs, most notably in the northwest
with three lines shown in color

RIVERS

a few river soundings are given
a lazy river meanders through
mapping of the interior is confined to rivers and lakes
near the junction of the... river and...
rivers and other waterways are especially attractive and detailed
shows settlement at mouth of river and surrounding wilderness
shows settlement at the confluence of the... and... Rivers
the Hudson River covers the eastern limit of this map
the rivers are attractively colored
the river winds across the page
the rivers which fill the interior are based on the accounts of...
the waterways are greatly exaggerated
traces the lucrative water route to markets
traces the river's course from its headwaters to the sea

SCALE

attempts to maintain equal scale throughout
large enough to show building detail
no scale is indicated

not drawn accurately to scale
some simplification of detail necessitated by the reduced size
with a large area fitting into a small map
with excellent, large scale detail of...

SIZE

designed to form one long plan
four sheets joined together as intended
huge map engraved on two plates
large, very detailed folding map, made up of twelve sections on a canvas backing
printed on three joined sheets
three sheets joined, each measuring...

SOURCE

detailed map from either... or..., probably the latter
from an undetermined edition of an atlas
from one of the great map publishing houses of Europe
possibly removed from an atlas

SURVEYS

a metes-and-bounds land survey
compiled chiefly from actual surveys
embracing surveys of...
extracted from land surveys
surveyed and mapped into six mile square townships

TEXT

as the long caption explains...
beneath the map are extensive interesting notes on...
bracketed by two columns of explanatory text
census figures assert that it is well populated
churches, schools and other buildings are identified singly
flanked by annotations
furnished with two pages of text
given in parentheses
includes text describing the history and geography of the area

large amount of information about... around border
Latin text on reverse side
least cluttered, easiest to read
lengthy notes on and marginal to...
numerous interesting notations
point-to-point mileages are listed
provides a precise verbal record
surrounded by related letterpress text
text at bottom explains origins of...
the key explains the symbols
the text includes this interesting statement
with a key to ten important locations
with copious information on...
with descriptive notes

TOPOGRAPHY

a vivid picture of the land emerges
clearly shows major topographical features
crude topographical plan of...
different types of terrain shown very clearly
European mapmakers followed these contours for decades
many physical features named
more emphasis on topography than...
much political and physical detail
presents important topographical data: waterways, rocky slopes, and farmlands
shows extensive river and mountain system
striking in its depiction of geological features
the topography receives minute treatment
topography is in a unique style
topography is shown with vague hachure lines
uses accurate contrast lines

INDEX

Notes

Notes

Notes